JOSEPH
From Prison to Palace

Other Biblical Character Studies by Walter C. Kaiser, Jr.

The Lives and Ministries of ELIJAH and ELISHA

ABRAHAM The Friend of God

JOSHUA A True Servant Leader

The Journey from JACOB to Israel

JOSEPH From Prison to Palace

Coming Soon

NEHEMIAH The Wall Builder

DAVID A Man After God's Own Heart

MOSES The Man Who Saw the Invisible God

SOLOMON The King with a Listening Heart

THE TWELVE The "Minor" Prophets Speak Today

ZECHARIAH The Quintessence of Old Testament Prophecy

DANIEL The Handwriting is on the Wall

RUTH The Moabite and the Providence of God

ESTHER God Preserves the Jewish Nation

JOSEPH
From Prison to Palace

Walter C. Kaiser, Jr.

Lederer Books
an imprint of
Messianic Jewish Publishers
Clarksville, MD 21029

Published by:
Lederer Books
An imprint of Messianic Jewish Publishers
6120 Day Long Lane
Clarksville, MD 21029

Distributed by:
Messianic Jewish Publishers & Resources
Order line: (800) 410-7367
lederer@messianicjewish.net
www.MessianicJewish.net

Table of Contents

Lesson 1

Joseph: From Prison to the Palace

Genesis 37–50

Joseph's story is unique. Few other stories in the Bible describe God's relationship with a person so intimately. However, this narrative has features in it that sound so familiar and so real that most of it could easily happened in our own day! So, let us immediately dig into this narrative and see why such a large block of Scripture was dedicated to Joseph.

Our Anger Against Others Can Block Our Thinking – 37:1–11

Our story begins with Jacob continuing to sojourn in the land of Canaan, but it quickly turns to the subject of his favorite son Joseph, a young man of only seventeen years of age, who shared in watching over the family's flocks with the sons of his father's two handmaids, Bilhah and Zilpah. Apparently, Joseph brought to his father a "bad report" about something his half-brothers had done or attempted, which meant the family name could be tarnished for some notorious act they had done in the neighborhood (v. 2).

Joseph should not just be called a tattletale for reporting his brothers' evil deed, for in the face of real evil, only a false pretense of honor requires us to hide wickedness when we see it. Scripture makes the point that when we see our brothers or sisters in the family, or even those who are part of us in the family of God, disgracing and hurting themselves, as well as others, we are to urge them to change their conduct and repent. If we are not in a position to so urge them, then we should inform those who are in a better position to follow up on this practice of evil with the proper response! Sin must be dealt with wherever it breaks out. It is also not clear why Joseph was shepherding with the sons of the handmaids, but it might indicate that the other brothers, who were sons of Leah, thought they were too high and mighty for the likes of this spoiled brat named Joseph!

The Cancer of Envy – 37:2–4

Joseph was the first son of Jacob's favorite wife Rachel, for he also was a child born in Jacob's later years. It was also true that Jacob loved Joseph "more that any of his other eleven sons, because he had been born to him in his old age" (v. 3). Moreover, Jacob made for him what appeared to be "a coat of many colors" (Hebrew *passim*, "of multicolored material") (v. 3b). But "when his brothers saw that their father loved [Joseph] more than any of them, they hated him and could not speak a kind word to him" (v. 4). Whether Jacob acted wisely in distinguishing Joseph from the rest of his brothers by this gift of this coat is unclear, but it is clear by now that Jacob had removed the birthright position from Reuben, the firstborn, and therefore had exposed Joseph to great envy and scorn.

Thus, the brothers hated Joseph so much that they were unable to speak a kind word to him (v. 4). This hatred was born out of deep envy and jealousy. Psalm 37:3–7 will later warn to "neither be envious," but rather trust in the Lord. Likewise, 1 Peter 2:1 will teach, "Lay aside all envies." This teaching is important, for those who are envious tend to make the other man's happiness their poison. So, we must beware of indulging in envy, for we have no idea where it might tend to lead us. In the case of the brothers, their envy had led them into hatred of Joseph. This envy gained such a degree of strength that it led to plots of murder against him. This endpoint for envy can become lethal!

The Cancer of Jealousy – 37:5–12

As if to add to the magnitude of the problem, Joseph had another dream in v. 9. In it, the sun, moon, and stars all bowed down to Joseph. That did it! This was getting to be too much for the brothers. The whole family got the meaning of this dream immediately without anyone interpreting it. Even Joseph's father, Jacob, "rebuked him" (Hebrew *ga'ar*, "to rebuke, speak insultingly to"), yet he kept (Hebrew *shamar*, "to guard, to keep") this matter in his mind (v. 11), for what if these dreams really were from God?

Whether Jacob fully understood all that God would do in Joseph's life over the next years is doubtful, because Jacob mourned the loss of his son, believing he had died. For 13 years Jacob mourned, and Joseph struggled. Apparently, it was necessary for God to take that long to perfect his instrument, for it was clear Joseph had a lot of pride and a lack of people-skills as he went through his teen years at home, especially with his brothers.

The theological point here is this:

> "Promotion comes not from the south, nor the east, nor from the west; it is the LORD that puts down one and sets up another; and who shall stay [hold back] his [the LORD's] hand or say to him, 'What doest thou?'" (Psalm 75:6–7; Daniel 3:35, KJV).

So, God had spoken once, yea twice, but as Job 33:14 reminded us, mortals still did not perceive that the Almighty was working his plan. The dreams had indeed come from God; they were not merely the musings or ravings of fancy by a teenager stuck on himself. And as with interpreting parables, so it is with interpreting dreams: Not every single object depicted must have a real-life counterpart. For example, Joseph's mother was already in the grave, so how was she expected to bow down to Joseph? Thus, she plays no part in its meaning.

Our Treachery Against Others, However, Cannot Frustrate the Plan of God – 37:12–28

The narrative changes in v. 12 as the brothers went off to pasture their father's flock near the town of Shechem. If, as we suspect, the Shechemite incident had already occurred (Simeon and Levi's murder of all the men of Shechem; see Gen. 34:25–29), then it might have been out of real concern for the safety of the brothers that Jacob sent his son Joseph to check on his brothers to see whether all was well with them! Thus, Joseph left the valley of Hebron and headed north for the vicinity of Shechem. Even though all the men of Shechem had been murdered, surely their surrounding neighbors would have desired revenge against Jacob's family, for this dastardly deed must have offended the consciences of many. No doubt this was the reason for Jacob's solicitous spirit for his sons' welfare at this time. Characteristically, Joseph obediently went off by himself to get the intelligence on how his brothers were doing.

When he arrived in the vicinity of Shechem, he did not find his brothers there; instead, an unidentified man found him wandering around in the field, who asked him, "What are you looking for?" (v. 15). When Joseph replied that it was his brothers he was seeking, the man volunteered that he heard them say, "Let's go to Dothan" (about

12–15 miles farther north) (v. 17). So, Joseph went off to Dothan, where he found his brothers. But when they saw him at a distance, they conspired to kill him (v. 18). Joseph was walking into a trap on his life!

"Here comes that dreamer," the brothers chorused. "Let's kill him and throw him into one of these cisterns and say that a ferocious animal, then we will see what comes of his dreams" (vv. 19–20). But where was a pit to be found that would be beyond the sight and omnipresence of God? With such a scheme, they intended to frustrate the word of the Lord and thus bring the counsels of the Almighty God to nothing! Did these brothers think they were a match for the Almighty? Did they think they could hide their sin? A possible excuse that they did not know that the dreams were from God was no justification for their murderous plan. Those who mock God's servants and their work will not be exempt from divine punishment by claiming that they didn't know that what they mocked was indeed from God. Moreover, their guilt is obvious, for now they attempt to cover their treachery by hatching a story built on lies. But lying lips are an abomination to the Lord (Proverbs 12:22). Of course, Jacob, their father, was not altogether without fault in this whole matter. He should have seen what was happening in his own family and taken action.

But when Reuben, Jacob's firstborn, heard about this plot, he knew he would not prevail in convincing his brothers not to murder Joseph, so he proposed a seemingly ghastlier plan—to throw him into a cistern in the wilderness (vv. 21–22). But all along, apparently, Reuben had in mind to return and rescue Joseph and bring him to his father to get into Jacob's good graces over the sexual prank he had previously pulled by going in and sleeping with

Jacob's concubine Bilhah (34:22). But Reuben's alleged rescue-plan of Joseph was not to be.

As soon as Joseph reached his brothers in Dothan, they stripped him of his coat of many colors, and then they cast him into an empty pit where there was no water (v. 23). Remarkably, having finished this part of their awful deed, they sat down to eat their meal, as if they had no conscience. But as they sat there, they looked up to surprisingly spot a caravan of Ishmaelites on their way to Egypt, their camels loaded with spices, balm, and myrrh (v. 25).

It seems it was Judah's turn to take the leadership in Reuben's absence, so he reasoned with his siblings, "What will we gain if we kill our brother and cover up his blood? Come, let us sell him to the Ishmaelites and not lay our hands on him; after all, he is our brother, our own flesh and blood" (vv. 26–27). The brothers agreed. So, they sold Joseph for twenty pieces of silver, and the Ishmaelites took him to Egypt (v. 28). The brothers must have thought that would be the last they would ever hear from this dreamer. He was gone for good!

Our Deceiving Others Cannot Inhibit God's Program of Grace – 37:29–36

Reuben returned only to learn, to his horror, that Joseph had been sold to the Egypt-bound Ishmaelite traders (v. 29). Jacob the deceiver would now be deceived by his own sons—using young goats to carry out the scheme. Jacob had taken the birthright from his brother Esau by using the skins of two "kid goats" (Hebrew `izzim, "kids of goats") to cover his arms in his mother's scheme to trick his sightless father Jacob (27:9). But now Jacob was the object of deception; his sons dipped Joseph's coat of many colors into the blood of "a kid of the goats" (Hebrew *se`ir `izzim*, "kid of the goats," v. 31). The men to whom Joseph was sold, however, also were Joseph's brethren, for the Ishmaelites and Midianites were sons of Abraham as well.

The boys boldly took Joseph's blood-soaked coat to their father and claimed they had found it. They pretended not to know it was Joseph's coat—but how many such coats worn in Canaan at that time were made of many colors? Liars! Of course, Jacob "recognized it" (v. 33). How cruel of these men to pull such a deed on their father! With what anguish it ripped up his soul, and for 13 long years his grief continued unabated, and the truth remained hidden. During those long years God was shaping and molding his servant Joseph in prison and then on the throne. Jacob refused to be comforted (v. 35), which must have made things hard around that Bedouin tent of that family. Meanwhile, Joseph was sold to one of Pharaoh's officials, Potiphar, the captain of the guard (v. 36).

Conclusions

1. Often our Lord takes his saints through trials and suffering, but he never deviates one iota from what he has planned; it is always in the end to do good to us.

2. Indeed, the Lord is wonderful in counsel and excellent in all his working out of his plans despite the movements of men to counter them!

3. What shall we say of the unresolved guilt and anger that resides in the hearts of men and women who have fallen into a similar pattern of envy?

4. What are they going through during this time if there is no forgiveness or reconciliation?

5. Was Jacob still carrying guilt because of what he had done to Esau?

Lesson 2

Joseph Resisting Sexual Temptation

Genesis 38:1–39:23

To some observers, the events in chapter 38 seem unrelated to the story of Joseph. Many commentators say the text intrudes on the main narrative. But v. 1 clearly wants us to note that these events took place "at that time," i.e., while Joseph was being sold to Potiphar in Egypt. Despite this clear linking together of this narrative with the Joseph story, all too many pay this chapter no attention, for in their opinion, it interrupts the flow of the story and doesn't mention anyone from the previous caste of Jacob's family except Judah.

In this narrative, however, Joseph, though younger than his brother Judah, steadfastly resisted the persistent advances of Potiphar's wife, while Judah easily gave-in to the sexual temptation set before him by his daughter-in-law Tamar in Gen. 39. The contrast here shows Joseph's greater moral and spiritual strength compared to his weaker brother, for Joseph doggedly resisted the temptation to have sex with Potiphar's wife.

There is no doubt an intentional literary connection between chapters 37 and 38 and between 38 and 39. For example, when Jacob's sons gave him Joseph's blood-soaked coat, they urged him to "examine it" (37:22). Similarly, when Tamar handed to Judah the items, he had given to her as a promise to later send a payment for her sexual services, she too later urged him to "identify" the items left as a pledge (38:25b), using in both cases the Hebrew verb *nakar*, "to recognize." The brothers dipped the coat in the "blood of a goat," while Judah promised to send to Tamar "a kid [from his] flock" (Hebrew *gedi ʾizzim*, 38:17) as payment. In addition to these literary connections of common words between these chapters, a half-dozen or more thematic parallels or contrasts can be identified to demonstrate that these chapters do have a connection with each other.[1]

By Steering Clear of the Traps Being Set Up for Us – 38:1–30

Judah apparently left his brothers, after they had sold Joseph to the Midianite traders, and headed for Adullam—a site in the Shephelah region of Canaan—to a town northwest of Hebron, where he pitched his tent near his friend Hirah, who hailed from the town of Adullam. We are not told who this man Hirah is, but he did not seem to be a positive influence on Judah. Judah seemed to be on a path that would take him, at this special time of sheep-shearing, another four miles to Timnah, where his flocks needed to be sheared. The fact that prior to this Judah had married a Canaanite woman, now deceased, is contrasted with the earlier patriarch Abraham and his obvious concern that his son Isaac, Jacob's father, should not marry a Canaanite woman! (Gen. 24:3). Where was Jacob when this marriage took place? We are not even given the name of this wife, only her father's name, "Shua." Scripture merely says Judah and this Canaanite woman "met," "married," and "cohabited" (38:2). She gave birth to three sons: Er, Onan, and Shelah (vv. 3–5). The account is so sparse of any further details that one can almost read unhappiness between the lines!

Judah got a wife for his oldest son, Er (perhaps meaning "watchful"), whose wife was named Tamar (meaning "date palm," v. 6), but this son "displeased the LORD," so God killed him (v. 7). There is no hint in the text as to why Er was wicked in God's sight. Neither is there any indication that Jacob mourned the death of his son Er.

---

1. For these further illustrations, see Victor P. Hamilton, *The Book of Genesis: Chapters 18–50 (New International Commentary on the Old Testament)*, Vol. 2 (Grand Rapids: Eerdmans, 1995), 431–432.

Instead, Jacob instructed his second son Onan ("strength," "vigor") to cohabit with Tamar, thus fulfilling his part in what is known in the Old Testament as "levirate marriage" (v. 8). Later Deuteronomy 25:5–10 stated that if brothers were living together and one of them who was married suddenly died without any children, then one of his surviving brothers was to take her or marry the widow and father a child by her, so the name of the deceased brother would not be forgotten. Should the brother-in-law decline to fulfill this obligation, he was to go the town's court, usually located in the gate of the town, where the city's elders met. There the widow was to appear, and the brother (who had refused to have intercourse), having rejected his duty as a Levir, was to publicly remove his shoe. The widow was to spit in his face, indicating the shame he had brought not only on himself but also on the town and nation! (See also Ruth's marriage to Boaz; Ruth 4:2–11. This practice continued even in Yeshua's day: Matthew 22:23–30; Mark 12:18–25; Luke 20:27–35).

The "levir" in this case was Onan, Judah's second-born. Onan did have sexual relations with Tamar, but he practiced coitus interruptus—instead of impregnating her, he deliberately withdrew from her as he was climaxing and let his semen drop to the ground! Thus, the term "onanism" came into being. This was not a form of birth control but of "inheritance control"; accordingly, this text is not to be read as a proscription of birth-control methods, nor as dealing directly with masturbation. Onan failed to own up to his responsibilities as a brother-in-law. He put his own interests in protecting the birthright for any sons he should later bear, rather than the interests of Er and Tamar. Moreover, what contributes to the heinousness of his sin was that Onan appeared to fulfill his responsibility of cohabiting with Tamar, only to fake full cohabitation and to indulge himself instead in the partial pleasure of the sexual act (vv. 9–10) while wasting the semen on the ground. Because of this evil, the Lord put him to death as well (v. 10b).

Judah instructed his widowed daughter-in-law to return to her father's household and live as a widow. But there is next to no evidence for such instructions for a widow. Apparently, Judah's third son, Shelah, was too young to have intercourse with Tamar, so Judah told her to wait for him to get older while she lived in her father's house. But by now, after having lost not just one but two sons to Tamar, along with having caused the family disgrace over speculation as to why both boys died, he appears to have had no intentions of risking his third son with this woman, so Tamar went off to live in her father's house, but she must have sensed she was being stonewalled by her father-in-law.

Judah headed to Timnah in time to oversee the work of his sheepshearers. His wife, as noted already, was not otherwise described except as the daughter of Shua (v. 12). Judah, however, had by now taken up with his friend the Adullamite named Hirah as they made their way to Timnah. Sheep-shearing was a time for major festivities (Hebrew *yom tob*, "good day)," in Israel, as seen in the narrative in 1 Samuel 25:8 where David sent his men to the place where Nabal was shearing his sheep, hoping for some free gifts at this festive time, only to be verbally abused by Nabal and denied any goods, despite how David and his men stood guard over this man's flock for so long. Where the town of Timnah was located is uncertain, but it appears to be in territory of the tribe assigned to Dan, which later became a center of Philistine occupation.

In the meantime, Tamar somehow heard that her father-in-law Judah was on his way to have his sheep sheared at Timnah (v. 13), so she set a trap for him; by now he had made it clear by his extended delay that he begrudged giving to her his son Shelah as a husband. Accordingly, she removed her widow's garments, veiled herself to conceal her identity, perfumed herself (to attract Judah) and took up a position just where the road forked off into two directions (v. 14).

As Judah came to that spot in the road, he saw her. He thought this woman was a prostitute, and she had covered her face, so he did not realize this was his none other than own daughter-in-law. Judah noticed the woman and fell headlong into her trap, for he immediately propositioned her: "Come, let me sleep with you" (vv. 15–16). Slyly, Tamar asked what Judah was willing to pay her for her services. Since Judah had left home without his American Express card, he said he would see that a young goat was sent to her (v. 17). Since credit cards were not in operation in that day, she asked what kind of assurance he could give that he was good for the promised goat! When he asked what she would like to have from him, she wisely suggested "his seal" (Hebrew *hotam*), along with its cord (*patil*), and the shepherd's "staff" (*matteh*) in his hand (v. 18). The seal usually consisted of an inscribed round stone about an inch or so long, with a hole through the center of it for the cord to go through it so it could be tied around its owner's neck. The seal had an identity inscription on it tantamount to a driver's license in that day, so the choice on her part was ingenuous. Judah had stalled all too long, so it was time he was publicly embarrassed.

Following his rendezvous, Judah sent Hirah the Adullamite with the goat as payment to look for this "prostitute," who by this time was being referred to simply as "the woman" (Hebrew *ha'ishsha*), and to retrieve his pledge items (v. 20). With the deception perfectly executed, Tamar had removed her veil and donned her widow's weeds once again (v. 19). As the Adullamite inquired of the townsmen where he could find the local prostitute (Hebrew *zonah*), they responded that there never had been such a person as a "cult/shrine prostitute" (Hebrew *qedehah*) (v. 21) in their town. When Hirah returned with the news that he was unable to find this woman or retrieve his pledge items, Judah said, "Let her keep what she has, or we will become a laughingstock" of the whole area (v. 23).

Three months later, Judah learned Tamar had become pregnant, and he became enraged and demanded in as righteous a manner as possible that she "be brought out and burned to death" (v. 24). But as she was being called out for her sin, she produced the pledge items he had lost. "I am pregnant by the man who owns these," she confessed, adding, "See if you recognize whose seal and cord and staff these are" (v. 25). Of course, Judah knew in an instant that he had been trapped but good! He meekly added: "She is more righteous than I, since I wouldn't give her to my son Shelah" (v. 26). Moreover, when the time for her to give birth came, behold, there were twin boys in her womb (v. 27). The midwife tied a scarlet thread to the wrist of the first one to stick his hand out of the womb (for she must have known that Tamar was pregnant with twins), but then he drew back, and his brother came out (v. 29). So, they named the first one "Perez" (Hebrew *parats*, "breach") and the other one "Zerah" (v. 30).

One must note that the ten-generation genealogy that concludes the book of Ruth begins with this same twin, named Perez, and concludes with David. Thus, in the genealogy of Yeshua in Matthew 1:1–17, Tamar is one of the first of the women mentioned there along with Rahab, Bathsheba, and Mary. Surely this is great evidence for the grace and mercy of God; but it was probably included to stop the gossip in Israel about Mary's virgin birth.

By Recalling God's Past Favor, Success, and Blessing – 39:1–6b

The God Whose Name Is Immanuel

We return to the story of Joseph, for he had been kidnapped and sold in Egypt to Potiphar, a high-ranking official of Pharaoh; indeed, one of his chief stewards (39:1). In fact, Potiphar was "captain of the guard," but he also was known from other sources as "chief of the executioners."

Now it appears that over the years, Joseph's brothers had completely forgotten about their pesky brother with his dreams, but God had not forgotten about him at all. Vv. 2 and 3 emphasize that "the LORD was with Joseph," for was he not one called "Immanuel," meaning "God with us"? Even though Joseph was experiencing affliction and suffering, that was no indication that God had abandoned him or that he hated him! Instead, as the New Testament will later indicate, "whom the Lord loves he disciplines" (Hebrews 12:6). Joseph may have been spoiled and pampered by his father Jacob, as the coat of many colors might indicate, but in other ways he showed himself to be very responsive in reacting positively to each new circumstance he was put in and each new call for obedience.

The God Who Blesses Us

So evident was the presence of God on Joseph's life that the Lord clearly blessed and prospered him in everything he did (v. 3). This work of God in Joseph's life was beyond anything that one could count as usual or normal. This blessing was so evident on this young man's life that even a godless and idol-worshiping man like Potiphar could tell there was something different about this boy. But this also made another point, for when God blesses his people Israel, even those who are connected with them are gifted with evidence of that same blessing (Gen. 12:3). Thus, Potiphar turned over everything in his household into Joseph's charge and keeping (v. 4). A later Scripture will teach a similar theology: A servant who is faithful in a few things will be put in charge of many things (Matthew 25:21). There could be no denying Joseph's faith in the Living God, any more than the Babylonian magistrates could deny Daniel's faith as he prayed every day three times daily (Daniel 6:10).

Did Joseph also have such faith because of what he saw in his father Jacob? True, Jacob had his problems and sins, but he also had great spiritual experiences: Did he not "see God face to face" (Gen. 32:27–35)? So changed was Jacob from that enormous encounter with God at Peniel that his own name was changed from "Jacob," "deceiver," to "Israel," "striver with God."

But this care and concern for those who have workers employed under them should be a believer's mark of the same type of trust, honor, and responsibilities extended to those men who work for them, for we must all give an account unto God in that final day as to how we treated those we were in charge of.

By Acting on the Fact That God Is Present and Sees Everything – 39:6c–20b

The Enemy Also Takes Notice of Successful Persons – 39:6c–8a

Potiphar was not the only person who was taken with Joseph's blessing and success that was now falling on all his possessions. So was Potiphar's wife watching; she "took notice of Joseph" (v. 7). But she had other reasons and motives for doing so. Perhaps her husband paid her no attention, so she was on the hunt for a man. Perhaps she wanted to get revenge, suspecting he was all too amorous with other women. But the Bible gives us what must be the most obvious reason for her notice: "Joseph was well-built and handsome." "Come to bed with me," she urged (vv. 6–7). As others have noted, "Her eyes ensnared her heart, and she lost all modesty, as well as every other virtue. She must have been lost to all sense of shame when she so barefacedly tempted Joseph to violate her chastity."[2] It seems few men could have resisted such a strong temptation from such a woman, for Joseph's older brother Judah had fallen for just such a trap. But Joseph held his integrity and would not let go of it, even though he could have rationalized the situation by saying that despite his dreams, God was no longer helping him. Yet he chose not to take that route.

Did Joseph need another trial on top of all that he had already been through? But the Lord knew what degree of troubles it would take to shape him and how long its pressure should continue.

The Enemy Intensifies the Temptation – 39:8b–20b

Joseph was in charge of everything Potiphar owned (v. 8b). Potiphar did not concern himself about any of the details of his household or his fields, for he had entrusted everything into the care and management of Joseph—except his wife! That is where Joseph and God drew the line. He told Potiphar's wife, "No one is greater in this house than I am. My master has withheld nothing from me except you because you are his wife. How then could I do such a wicked thing [by making love to you] and sin against God?" (v. 9). This was not as easy to say and do on paper as it was in real life, for Joseph would have had the opportunity and the occasion to yield to Potiphar's wife's blandishments. He could have falsely reasoned that after all, he was in a different culture, and life had been hard on him in many ways, so why not indulge in a little bit of fun.

––––––––––––––––––––

2. George Lawson, *The Life of Joseph* (Carlisle, PA: The Banner of Truth Trust, 1988), 33.

The temptation was more than an occasional invitation; in fact, it was persistent, and went on "day after day" (v. 10). It was clearly verbally spoken, "Come to bed with me!" It too was physical, for she "caught him by his cloak" (v. 11), but Joseph let go of his cloak and ran outside the house (v. 12). This was a desperate woman who was intent on getting what she wanted when she wanted it. However, some 400 years later, Moses would write in the Ten Commandments, "You shall not commit adultery," nor should one "covet your neighbor's wife" (Exodus 20:14, 17).

This would be not just a sin against Potiphar and his wife; it would be a sin against God. God sees everything. Moreover, he had chosen Joseph and called him to do a special task. It had been God all along who had been giving him success and blessing all the work of his hands. How could he sin against God? He could and would not. This was not a sin of sin between two consenting adults; no, it was a sin also against God!

The Aftermath of Frustrating Evil – 39:13–20b

It is one thing to resist evil and be rewarded for doing so, but it is an altogether different situation to resist evil and suffer for refusing to take the evil path. From a human standpoint, it seems Joseph paid a high price for being faithful to his conscience and his knowledge that our Lord is an omniscient Lord. When this lascivious wife saw that Joseph had fled her grasp, and in doing so, had left her holding his cloak, she deviously called all of her household servants and with an impudent face lied to them, saying, "Look, this Hebrew has been brought to us to make sport of us. He came in here to sleep with me, but I screamed. When he heard me scream for help, he left his cloak beside me and ran out of the house" (vv. 14–15).

Never should Joseph have been alone with this woman in the house (v. 10), but she contrived it to be otherwise (v. 11). Therefore, she represented the situation to her husband in such a way that he would be honor-bound by the laws of marriage to make an example out of Joseph in front of the rest of the help in his household. But he did not execute Joseph, for he no doubt knew by now his wife's weaknesses. But if she were so distraught by what had happened, why did she pretend to be too modest to say plainly what Joseph had done to her?

God's hand of protection was on Joseph. God still had plans for Joseph, and this silly woman was not going to get her way by making up a fake story about what had gone on between them!

By Relying on the Faithfulness of God in the Future -39:20c–23

Joseph was thrown into prison as a result of the fake story told by his deceptive wife. But God did not forsake Joseph; "the LORD was with him." (v. 21a). By now the pressure seems to be mounting up, for this young lad had been debased by his own brothers, sold into Egypt for the going price of a slave in that day, accused by Potiphar's wife, and imprisoned by him. Amazingly, however, because of God's care and presence, Joseph was "granted favor in the eyes of the prison warden" (v. 21). Once again, so dependable was Joseph in carrying out his duties that the warden made him responsible for all that was done in the prison (v. 22). In fact, the warden paid no attention to anything that was under Joseph's oversight, because "the LORD was with Joseph and gave him success in whatever he did" (v. 23). How great are the mercies and blessings that come from our God!

Conclusions

1. Is it not true that we are most vulnerable to temptation when we are the most successful?

2. If we think we are able to stand firm in the face of any attack, we must be careful that we do not fall (1 Corinthians 10:12). "Seek first the kingdom of God and his righteousness and [then] all these things shall be added unto you" (Matthew 6:33).

3. The best defense against a charged wrong is a good offense—one provided by the God, who is always with us to bless us and to prosper us in all our ways, especially when we have chance to bless Jewish people who are called by God to be the center of his plan.

4. Much temptation can be avoided by steering clear of all incentives, occasions, and offers to sin. Psalm 1 says "Blessed is the person who does not walk in the counsel of the ungodly, stand in the way of sinners, or sit in the seat of mockers."

5. Is it not true that "In all things God works for the good of those who love him" (Romans 8:28)?

Lesson 3

Joseph: Interpreting Dreams
for a Pair of Jailbirds

Genesis 40:1–23

By now, some eleven years had passed since Joseph was sold by his brothers to the Midianite merchants; he was seventeen when Jacob gave him his coat of many colors (37:2), and thirty years old when Pharaoh put him in charge of all Egypt (41:46). And if the events in chapter 40 took place two years before he was made prime minister (41:1), then we can reasonably conclude that some eleven years had passed in the interim since he was carted off to Egypt.

Even though Joseph had been given a good deal of freedom during most of those two years in prison, at least his initial time was especially difficult. As Psalm 105:17–19 recounts:

> And he sent a man before them—Joseph, sold as a slave. They bruised his feet with shackles, his neck was put into irons, till what he foretold came to pass, till the word of the LORD proved him true.

Just how long Joseph endured such affliction is not known to us, but it certainly was long enough for the shackles to leave bruises on his feet, no doubt along with other wounds. But eventually Joseph was rewarded with a degree of freedom, for he was assigned two of the king's servants who had somehow offended the king and were summarily thrown into prison. We are not told their names. We do know they served Pharaoh as his cupbearer and chief baker (40:1), which were quite responsible positions in the administration of the nation of Egypt. The butler/cupbearer was an especially trusted servant, for he tasted the king's food and drink to make sure no one was attempting to poison the king. Likewise, the baker had to be a trusted servant, for he oversaw all the royal food preparation. Should attempts be made on Pharaoh's life, these two men would be among the first to feel its sad effects in their bodies! The two of them were in prison because in some major way they had really ticked off Pharaoh, so they were stripped of their jobs and put in prison. We will investigate more later, but both men had dreams while they were incarcerated. Before going forward in this narrative, we will discuss the topic of dreams in the Bible.

Dreams and Visions in the Ancient Near East

Dreams and visions are a real part of the biblical narrative. God can break into the consciousness of mortals at any time, day and night. One thing is certain: In Scripture, God is pleased to send dreams and visions fairly frequently to give his divine revelation to mortals. Not all dreams in the ancient world were of divine origin. But it did seem that God occasionally sent dreams when the publication of his word had gotten scarce or rare (1 Samuel 3:1).

Often the word of the Lord came at night, as it did to the prophet Nathan, in that fabulous prophecy marked for David in 2 Samuel 7:4, 17; and 1 Chronicles 17:3, 15, just as it had come at night to Gideon (Judges 6:25; 7:9) and to the prophet Isaiah, "My soul yearns for you in the night, my spirit earnestly seeks you" (26:9). However, the prophet Hosea warned that [false] prophets stumbled at night (4:4), and Micah likewise warned of the absence of revelation at night, so again, discretion was needed in all these instances.

In a good number of dreams, God speaks directly, as in the dreams given to Joseph, which frequently needed no interpreter; the brothers and Jacob got the meaning without the aid of an interpreter

(Gen. 37:8). The same was true of the dream given about Gideon's enemies (Judges 7:13). Other dreams, however, were metaphorical, and did need an interpreter—such as "Pharaoh's cows" (Gen. 41) and the dreams of the "three branches" in the butler and baker's dreams (Gen. 40:5–19).

In the ancient world, a favorite way of consulting God, or inquiring of one's idols, was to go sleep in the temple of that god during the night in order to gain a dream. Such dreams were called "incubation dreams." Solomon is a good example of this process, for one night he slept at the great high place in Gibeon in order to receive his dream and instructions from God (1 Kings 3:4, 5). But one had to do this with care, for some forms of making inquiries of God or of other supernatural sources were off-limits, such as the desire to consult with the spirit of a person who had died. Scripture called this an abomination (Leviticus 19:31; Deuteronomy 18:11). Moreover, some dreams were not just benign, for they did scare and shock Job's comforter Eliphaz, as he said he found out by experience (Job 7:14). And for those who misinterpreted their dream or vision, often the source of this confusion was a lying spirit (1 Kings 22:22–23).

God used dreams and visions to communicate his word to men and women. Sin, however, could be a great blockage and when the word of God became rare and scarce, for that loss of revelation could signal an abandonment by God of that generation or culture.

By Bearing Up Patiently While Waiting for God's Deliverance – 40:1–4

Eleven years had passed since Joseph had been sold into Egypt. Much of that time Joseph may have spent in prison. He likely wondered whatever had happened to the dreams he had dreamt; but the text never said he ever raised the issue.

Two of the men on the staff of Pharaoh suddenly were thrown into the same prison where Joseph was being detained. It was from this incident of what seemed to be remote circumstances that God began to work Joseph's deliverance from prison and the fulfillment of what he had dreamed almost thirteen years ago. The Lord knew Joseph was not guilty of the crimes for which he had been thrown into prison. Despite how things appeared to be, God, in his infinite wisdom, had been working all along to position Joseph for the fulfillment of what he had revealed long ago. The only thing Joseph knew was that Potiphar had answered his wife's plea and therefore had Joseph bound and committed to prison (39:20). Joseph had done nothing to deserve incarceration. But again, the Lord "showed him kindness and granted him favor in the eyes of the prison warden (39:21). At first Joseph was confined under the "captain of the guard," but then he was freed of his fetters and appointed as the warden's delegate to take charge of and serve the royal cupbearer and chief baker, who Pharaoh had ordered into the same prison (40:3).

The charges against these men had been permitted by God as part of his infinite, but at times mysterious, plan. But in the end, these events were all part of God's plan to rescue Joseph and use him in ways he could never have imagined. Surely this should remind us that if the wrath of a king was to be feared (Proverbs 19:12), should believers not all the more fear our Lord, who is all-powerful. (Matthew 10:28).

Nevertheless, through these thirteen long years, Joseph did not grow bitter against God or his circumstances; he must have continued to believe that what God had said to him in the days of his youth was still true and would certainly take place, despite how dark things looked for the present. Unlike the other two men, who may or may not have been guilty as charged, Joseph had God's presence to cheer him each day. So even though Joseph had been treated unfairly, he had ministering to him the confidence of a clear conscience before God and the mighty sense that God was present with him in his trials. As George Lawson reminds us:

> Let not those who are in some degree removed from sickness, though not restored to prefect health, repine that it is not with them as in former times. ... [Sometimes] troubles are greatly alleviated by the remembrances of greater troubles. ... Let us always cheerfully accommodate ourselves to those circumstances in which Divine Providence is pleased to place us. They are unworthy to be exalted who cannot bear to be humbled.[1]

By Taking Every Opportunity to Demonstrate Our Faith – 40:5–19

The Night the Two Former Officials Dreamed

Usually, dreams are unimportant and fade quickly. Yet there are occasions where God has given to mortals an intimation of what his will is for us or for others as we sleep. Of course, this condition was more common in times when the written revelation of the divine will was not as available or complete as it is today. Even so, as Job commented in Job 33:14, "God speaketh once, yea twice, yet man perceiveth it not" (KJV).

When Joseph came to his two charges in the morning (40:6), the men were sad and dejected. Come to think of it, since Joseph was in the same situation, why do we not hear that he too was dejected and sad—he had more than just trivial reasons to let his demeanor sink into despondency. When Joseph inquired what was the reason for their disquiet, both men replied, "We both had dreams ... but there is no one to interpret them" (v. 8). In the outside world, they could have appealed to a charmer or a magician to interpret; but what were they to do here in a prison?

---

1. George Lawson, *The Life of Joseph* (Carlisle, PA: The Banner of Truth Trust, 1988), 49–51.

It was time for Joseph to witness. He still believed that the Lord who gave the dreams could also give their interpretation. Joseph believed the dreams would be fulfilled; of this he showed no doubt. God would do what he had said! In fact, he began by informing these Egyptians that "interpretations belong to God," and he said, "Tell me your dreams" (v. 8).

The Two Dreams

The cupbearer went first. It was not strange that he should dream of grapes, wine, cups and putting them into Pharaoh's hands. He saw a vine with three branches. Soon after it budded and the grapes came, the butler squeezed the ripened grapes into a cup and offered it to Pharaoh (vv. 9–11).

In short order, Joseph was given the interpretation to the butler's dream. He declared the three branches meant three days, for in three days the king's cupbearer would be restored to the position he had just been dismissed from, and once again he would serve Pharaoh. There is no way human wisdom could have discerned that those three branches meant three days! This was a result of divine interpretation. Joseph learned that from God.

Joseph took the occasion to describe his own imprisonment to the butler: "I was forcibly carried off from the land of the Hebrews, and even here I have done nothing to deserve being put in a dungeon." He earnestly requested that the butler return the favor by mentioning his case to Pharaoh when he was restored to his former position (vv. 14–15).

Now it was time for the baker to relate his story, for he had been listening to all that Joseph had to say to the butler. Since it had gone so well for him, the baker ventured, "I too had a dream: On my head were three baskets of bread. In the top basket were all kinds of baked goods for Pharaoh, but the birds were eating them out of the basket on my head" (vv. 16–17). Given the details he offered, it is no wonder he was somewhat hesitant to share his dream, for fear it would not go as well for him as it had for the cupbearer. Of course, certain elements in the two dreams were similar, but other details were quite dissimilar.

The baker's interpretation came just as quickly and succinctly as had the butler's interpretation. Joseph announced: "The three baskets are three days" (v. 18). So far, things were going well, for that was how the butler's interpretation began. But then things got bad. Joseph declared, "Within three days, Pharaoh will lift off your head and impale your body on as pole. And the birds will eat away your flesh" (v. 19). That was not what the baker had hoped for, to say the least!

By Receiving Encouragement From the Immediate Proofs of God's Love for Us – 40:20–23

The point of all of these details was this: "Just as Joseph had said to them in his interpretation" (v. 22), so it happened. What a great encouragement this was to Joseph, who no doubt by this time needed a good boost after all he had been through for all these years. Had the cupbearer been raised the least bit of doubt in Pharaoh's mind, you could be sure he would not have pardoned this man, for his life hung on his making the right decision.

The third day turned out to be Pharaoh's birthday (v. 20). The cupbearer was restored, but he forgot Joseph's plea that he relates his situation to Pharaoh (v. 23). He failed to remember the kindnesses Joseph had shown him and his accurate prediction as to what would take place!

Scripture, however, warns that in the last days before the second coming of our Lord, many will be ungrateful, unthankful, and unkind (2 Timothy 3:1–5). They will love only themselves, not God.

Conclusions

1. Believers often must endure hardships and sufferings as good soldiers of Yeshua (2 Timothy 2:3).

2. We must be careful not to let bitterness toward others capture our lives and turn into bitterness toward God for the pain we sometimes suffer.

3. The psalmist will ask in Psalm 43:5, "Why are you cast down, O my soul? Why are you disquieted within me? Hope in God, for I shall yet praise him for the help of his countenance."

Lesson 4

Controlling the Destinies of Nations

Genesis 41:1–57

Joseph received his first ray of hope for a release, and perhaps his first opportunity for an answer to his prayers, from his request to the cupbearer, whose dream he had just correctly interpreted as promising this butler's release from prison (40:23; 41:1). But he must have waited day after day for some word after the butler left the prison, for the man forgot all about his promise to Joseph. So much for human promises! Joseph likely thought that as soon as Pharaoh heard from the cupbearer of the wrongful incarceration, he would immediately get the attention he needed. He would get relief from the past eleven years of his troubles. But no word came! In fact, Joseph's waiting went on for two more solid years. Did that mean that now Joseph would be on the verge of giving up all hope?

One might think that since God had given Joseph the ability to know when someone else would be released from their bondage, surely God would have revealed to Joseph when he too would be freed. But it was not so; Joseph had to continue to have faith and to place his hope solidly in his Lord, for no help was coming from any human sources! Where was God in all of this turmoil? Didn't he answer prayer anymore?

God Used Humanity's Frustrated Understandings to Prepare the Way for His Purposes and Plans – 41:1–8

As far as we can tell, two full years had by now passed since the cupbearer had been reinstated and been the benefactor of Joseph's positive dream-interpretation, but Joseph reaped no benefit for all his labors in prison. It might have been two more added years that Joseph had to endure imprisonment from Potiphar. But a new moment did come—when Pharaoh dreamed two dreams that once again might well have come on his birthday. But from Joseph's point of view, the intervening years were the same old happenings with no hope for deliverance from the drudgery of prison life. Proverbs 13:12, "Hope deferred makes the heart sick." No doubt in Joseph's mind, this delay had gone on too long. Few men would have been more patient than Joseph, except perhaps King David as he waited for his turn to take over the reins of government in Israel. Yet find even David cried out to God,

> "How long, O LORD? Will you forget me forever? How long will you hide your face from me? How long must I wrestle with my thoughts?" (Psalm 13:1–2a)

Joseph may well have felt he was spending the best years of his life in jail. However, God continued calling Joseph to be patient in the trials he was going through, for surely the Lord knew the most appropriate moment to interpose his help and release him. In the meantime, Joseph was being called, as we often are called in similar trials and situations, to give thanks to God for the staying power of his word, a word that gives both Joseph and us the grounds for our hope for the future.

Pharaoh's Dreams – 41:2–7

Pharaoh's dreams may seem like a jumble of incoherent views on agricultural life in Egypt, but when interpreted, they made a lot of sense. Who would ever have imagined a dream of cows emerging from the Nile River or about ears of grain that ate up each other's heads? These were not the typical kind of dreams a mortal usually had about the future; such dreams as these had to have come from God! God withheld the meaning of Pharaoh's dream until it was revealed to Joseph, unlike his brothers, who immediately understood the dreams that involved them. No, Pharaoh needed someone to interpret for him the events he saw. Had either dream been so simple that the local wise-men and enchanters could explain it, God's reason for sending the dreams would have been missed. God had a greater purpose for the dreams in the form he sent them; he wanted to use the man he had prepared to interpret this dream, Joseph, to do so. Nor was the timing off, for God sent the time just when the butler finally recalled his promise to Joseph. Talk about the providence of God—wow!

Pharaoh's dream, as told to Joseph, was this: There came up out of the Nile River seven sleek and fat cows to graze in a meadow by the river (41:2). Seven more followed, but this second set of seven cows was ugly and gaunt. They stood beside the other cows, and the ugly cows devoured the sleek, fat cows (v. 3). With that, Pharaoh woke up! I imagine we too would have awakened when we saw what these cattle were doing!

The king fell asleep again, and God gave him a second dream. Seven heads of healthy and good grain were growing on a single stalk. These were followed by seven other grains, but they were thin and scorched as a result of the strong east wind (vv. 5–6). The thin grains began to swallow up the healthy, full grains. Once more, Pharaoh woke up (v. 7). Can you blame him? I suppose he felt there must be a "grain of truth" somewhere in these dreams, but for the life of him, he had no idea what that meaning could be!

Pharaoh's Frustration – 41:8

Pharaoh was one troubled monarch. By morning he was at his wit's end. What did all of this mean? Why was it happening in his own Nile River? Why were the cows in the river anyway? It would be full of their natural predators swimming about. All this was confusing!

Naturally, Pharaoh sent for his wise men, magicians, and enchanters of all types, and he described the dream. It was still vivid in his mind, but they could not "milk" any meaning from these descriptions! None of these charlatans could offer an interpretation. These so-called wise men knew as little as Pharaoh did about the God of the universe and his plan and will for mortals and the nations. They needed the entrance of God's word to give them light. Failing that aid, they were clueless.

God Used Persons to Explain to the Nations His Divine Plan – 41:9–36

The Cupbearer Remembers He Forgot to Inform Pharaoh – 41:9–13

In the midst of the royal crisis, the chief butler finally remembered the promise he had made to Joseph long ago, and he said, with some contrition, "Today I am reminded of my shortcomings" (v. 9). He then explained how Pharaoh had been angry with two of his servants, the butler and chief baker, and imprisoned them (v. 10). Both of them had a dream on the same night, but what were their chances of obtaining an interpretation in prison? Fortunately, there was incarcerated with them a "young Hebrew," a servant of the captain of the guard, who told both men the exact meaning of their dreams. Surprisingly, the cupbearer recalled, "things turned out exactly as he interpreted them to us: I was restored to my position, and the other man was impaled" (vv. 12–13).

An Interpretation Summoned – 41:14–32

Pharaoh immediately sent for Joseph, so he was quickly brought out of his imprisonment setting, where he quickly shaved, changed his clothes, and was brought before Pharaoh (v. 14).

The king of Egypt began, "I had a dream, and no one can interpret it, but I have heard it said of you that when you hear a dream you can interpret it" (v. 15). But as most readers of Scripture know, it is only common language that when the Bible says that things were done by certain persons, it only means that those who merely said, or they did those things; it really was God who actually accomplished and carried out what the person claimed to have said or done!

In this case, though, Joseph was clear: "I cannot do [the interpretation of your dream] ... but God will give Pharaoh the answer he desires" (v. 16). Joseph gave God all the credit. The years of trials and confinement were now making themselves evident as the fruit of all Joseph had experienced came to the fore. Previously, there had been a day in which perhaps a prideful young man would have grabbed the credit for himself. But now it was clear why Potiphar and the prison warden continued to be impressed by Joseph's demeanor. No doubt they were seeing a direct connection between the God this young man worshiped and the success he enjoyed. But more than that, only those men and women who are deeply sensitive to their own unfitness to serve God are fit to declare the counsels of God. But those who take all the praise to themselves of what they do in the service of God are liable to receive the punishments of God.

It seemed that Pharaoh, in the meantime, had not forgotten one word of his dreams, for he began to carefully recite his dreams for Joseph (vv. 17–24). In fact, Pharaoh expressed himself a bit stronger this time as he contrasted seven of the cows who first came up out of the river as being well-favored with seven more cows that came up after them as being ill-favored.

Joseph began his interpretation by observing that the Pharaoh's two dreams were actually one and the same (v. 25). The seven good cows, Joseph continued, were "seven years," just as the seven bad cows were another "seven years" (v. 26). The same meaning was attached to the good grains and the bad grains (v. 27). By these dreams, Joseph said, "God has shown Pharaoh what he is about to do. Seven years of great abundance are coming throughout the land of Egypt, but seven years of famine will follow them" (vv. 28b–30). Joseph warned that the famine would be so severe that the memories of the seven good years would soon be forgotten (v. 31). And the reason God gave the dream in two separate forms was so that he would see that the matter was firmly decided and duly "established" (Hebrew *nakon*) by God and that God would soon bring all of this to pass (v. 32).

Joseph did not hesitate to begin his interpretation without any prolonged prologue. He didn't utter any mystical incantation or use any type of pagan practice, as the magicians typically would have done. He simply and succinctly began with the interpretation of both dreams. His point of witness was just as clear and just as direct. Had Joseph come before Pharaoh, say, two years earlier, when the butler was released promised to remember him by telling Pharaoh of his story, there likely would have been no need for Joseph's help. In that instance, his appeal could have fallen flat with no relief from prison. But now in this clear example of God's providence, he had made this all come together at just the right moment. God must have been working the behind the scenes for those thirteen years while also preparing Joseph as a better candidate for his plan and will.

Advice Given to Appoint an Overseer – 41:33–36

Now that Joseph had solved the meaning and significance of these things, it would be best if some actions were taken to implement the matters raised in these dreams, Joseph advised. Pharaoh should look for a wise and discerning man (v. 33). That man should be in charge and empowered to appoint commissioners over the whole land of Egypt. One-fifth of all that was harvested in Egypt during those seven good years should be collected by the king and set aside to be stored in the cities of Egypt. The food should be held in reserve during those seven years for the seven years of famine, as the God of the universe said were coming (v. 36).

God Used Prepared People to Rule Over the Nations – 41:37–57

Pharaoh liked Joseph's plan, as did all of his officialdom's leaders (v. 37). But Pharaoh also added, "Can we find anyone like this man [Joseph], one in whom is the spirit of God?" (v. 38) There must have been complete agreement, for Pharaoh continued,

"Since God has made this known to you, there is no one so discerning and so wise as you. You shall be in charge of my

> palace, and all my people are to submit to your orders. Only with respect to the throne will I be greater than you." (vv. 39b–40).

Joseph stood before Pharaoh and his leaders confidently, but without overconfidence in himself. He consistently gave all the glory to God for his ability to interpret these dreams, as well as the advice to store up grain for the coming famine. Joseph said he in his own strength could not do whatever he was being called to do, but he was just as sure that God could and that God himself would empower with divine help the persons he had called to do this task! This principle was not an excuse by Joseph to argue for laziness on his part, or a disclosure of indecisiveness. It was a testimony that he depended wholly and totally on the call and help of the Sovereign God.

Pharaoh was king in the land of Egypt, but he empowered Joseph enormously. He decreed, "Without your word, no one will lift hand or foot in all Egypt" (v. 44b). He had put Joseph "in charge of the whole land of Egypt" (v. 41b). Pharaoh removed his signet ring, which was needed to authorize any action in Egypt, and he put it on Joseph's finger, for Joseph was now in charge of all the affairs of state. He dressed Joseph in robes of fine linen and put a gold chain around his neck (v. 42). Pharaoh had him ride in his personal chariot as his second-in-command (to which Joseph no doubt attached a license plate reading *"#2"*) and ordered the people to "bow the knee" (Egyptian *'abrek*) in advance of Joseph's arrival anywhere in Egypt (v. 43). Joseph was also given a new name, "Zaphenath-Paneah," and a wife named Asenath, the daughter of Potiphera, priest of On (v. 45). All of this was happening to Joseph who had just reached 30 years of age (v. 46). God also gave Joseph and his wife two sons: one named "Manasseh," meaning "one who causes to forget [all the harsh treatment over the years]," and the other named "Ephraim," meaning "God has made me fruitful."

The seven years of plenty came to an end and the seven years of famine took over as Joseph had foretold. His task called for enormous strength and help from the Lord. The collection of grain became one gigantic storehouse operation, for in every city huge amounts of grain, raised from grain grown in the environs of that city, were piled up against the expected seven years of famine that were to come. The surplus of grain became so huge that Joseph stopped keeping records any longer of the total amount (v. 49).

When the famine did hit, Joseph was faced with an equally huge task: distributing the grain. As the famine began, the Egyptians began to plead with Pharaoh to help them, but he simply replied, "Go to Joseph and do what he tells you" (v. 55). Thus, young as Joseph was (as he began at only 30 years of age), he was now tasked with handling a "world problem," all without any prior intensive and mentored course on managing and feeding of the Near Eastern World. The words "put in charge" have frequently occurred in this chapter in experience after experience of Joseph, but this time he was really put in charge. But Scripture never says that Joseph complained. Instead, he handled the demands of the job with its prestige and power extremely well without succumbing to pride or demands for recognition.

Conclusions

1. God can teach Joseph, and all of the rest of us, the lessons that will help us avoid pride and selfish demand for position and recognition. Proverbs warns of seven things the Lord hates: haughty eyes, a lying tongue, hands that shed innocent blood, a heart that rushes to wicked schemes, feet that are quick to rush to evil, a false witness and a person who stirs up dissension (Proverbs 6:16–19).

2. God can shape us into the vessel he needs to serve him with a preparatory course of study and living that will enable us to perform well.

3. Those who honor God, God will honor them.

4. The providence of God can be vividly seen in the drama of what happens to Joseph during his 13 years of imprisonment.

Lesson 5

Joseph: Awakening Guilty Consciences

Genesis 42:1–38

By this time, the famine was growing severe not only in Egypt, but throughout the Near East. By now it had spread throughout the known world (41:57). Accordingly, Joseph's former homeland of Canaan had been hard-hit by the same seven years of scarcity. Surprisingly, however, word soon spread that there was grain available in Egypt, so naturally Jacob sent his ten sons to Egypt to buy food for the family. But God would use this natural calamity to bring Jacob's sons face-to-face with the brother they had first intended to kill, then ended up selling to a band of Midianite merchants on their way to trade in Egypt.

This episode in the life of Joseph raises the theological issue of forgiving someone who has wronged us, even though in many cases that person may have not yet acknowledged his or her part in any wrongdoing or even sought forgiveness of the party they had wounded. This means our willingness to forgive must not be necessarily predicated on the offender's having already asked our forgiveness. What all too often happens is that when the one who has wronged us comes face-to-face with us, our first instinct is to retaliate and make them feel some of the hurt that we endured in the meantime for all that had taken took place since that encounter.

In this case, the time that has passed by in the interim was some 22 years! Joseph had not only been separated for that time from his father, his home and all the familiar surroundings he had had in his teenaged years, but he had had no way of contacting his father to let him know he was alive! There was, however, no doubt Joseph's brothers had treated him cruelly. This is not to say Joseph was totally without fault, for in most of these situations it takes two persons to make an argument. But we certainly can say that Joseph did not deserve the total load of evil he had suffered so heartlessly from his own flesh and blood.

Still, Joseph did manage to evidence a loving attitude toward his brothers; Scripture does not suggest he bore any grudges against them, nor did he ever, in all those years, exhibit a desire to get even with them. It seems God had brought healing to his heart and soul, so that the plan of God to which he had been called was one so amazing, it was beyond anything he could have imagined. Perhaps this may have enabled him to forget all the misery that had overtaken him in Egypt. The comfort of God, then, no doubt brought healing to his afflicted soul.

Some two years into the famine, his ten brothers suddenly showed up wanting to buy grain, and it must have brought back some painful memories to his mind. But amazingly, Joseph deported himself in a wise and kindly way. He could have thought this was his opportunity finally to show his brothers that what he had been through was no fun at all! Now that he was in control, his brothers were at his mercy. He could have thrown them into prison on some trumped-up charge, but he didn't. He could have refused to sell them grain, for he had the authority. But instead, Joseph became a model for us to follow when we too have been treated in unfair, unkind, and cruel ways.

Try to picture what crossed Joseph's mind when all of a sudden, who should show up to buy grain—none other than his ten brothers, who had so cruelly wronged him. There they were, standing in front of him. Obviously, since Joseph was only seventeen years of age when they last saw him and now he was almost forty, the brothers did not recognize who it was they were dealing with. And what did Joseph think when he saw ten men from Canaan bow down low before him exactly as he had dreamed over twenty years ago? Wasn't it in his first dream, where he was in the field with his brothers, when Joseph's sheaf "rose and stood upright," and his brothers' sheaves gathered around him and "bowed down to it" (37:7)? And wasn't it in a second dream where "the sun and moon and eleven stars were bowing down" to him (37:9)? True, Joseph had naïvely goaded his brothers by relating these dreams to them, but they also had a prophetic and supernatural significance, even though the brothers thought he was just some kind of spoiled, boastful, and proud brat who needed to be silenced.

But now, 22 years later, his dreams were all taking place right before his eyes. All of a sudden it became clear why God had allowed him to be sold into Egypt. The fact that God had used the brothers' wrongdoing did not mean that what they did was not wrong and deserving of God's rebuke and judgment, for it was. But the purposes of our Lord are so exacting and so all-embracing that those plans can work both what is good as well as what is bad. It was not up to Joseph to try to set the wrongs right by retaliating for all they had done to him; justice belongs to God. But let us look at this text on guilt and forgiveness in more depth.

Through the Circumstances of Life – 42:1–5

Canaan, the land the Lord had promised to be the land of milk and honey, suddenly did not reflect the same bounty. This would not be the first or the last famine this land of promise would face, which otherwise was potentially endowed to provide an abundance of food. But if self-sufficiency had promoted some unwanted pride, as seen in Jacob's family, the famine would help temper such boastfulness. Fortunately, Jacob got word that grain was available in Egypt at this time, but why God had not chosen to inform Jacob ahead of time of this famine or where grain would be available? Was it because that the family was not living the way God wanted them to live? The text is silent on this issue. Nor did heaven choose to inform Jacob that the grain in Egypt was all due to God's provision through Jacob's favorite son Joseph! This too had been left unrevealed.

In the midst of the famine, the eleven brothers sat idle "look[ing] one upon another" (42:1). But the times called for action, but it appeared that any resolve of getting-up and getting-going had been removed from the heart of the boys, who were suffering from a heavy load of guilt. It was left to their father Jacob to urge the boys to get going down to Egypt and to buy grain for the family or else they all were going to die (v. 2).

Meanwhile, Joseph had managed a super crop-storage system during the seven years of abundance in Egypt, and it was now two years into the seven years of famine. So why had Joseph allowed his father to extend his suffering for this added time when the good news that he was still alive and well would have brought real joy to Jacob's aged heart? How did the news of grain in Egypt come to Jacob? And why did he send his ten sons to buy grain when he probably had hundreds of menservants he could have chosen from to send on the family's behalf? Or were his sons to be more trusted or perhaps needed to identify their heritage in order to purchase grain? In any case, it was Joseph's ten brothers, who in God's providence, were sent to buy grain (v. 3). There was one important exception, however: "Jacob did not send Benjamin, Joseph's brother, with the others, because he was afraid that harm might come to him" (v. 4). Off the boys went to Egypt, but without Benjamin, the son of

Jacob's favorite wife Rachel, for the text tells us explicitly that "the famine was [even] in the land of Canaan" (v. 5). However, the time for fulfilling Joseph's dreams was now drawing near—the brothers had once scorned the dreams, and now they would be the main characters in their fulfillment!

Through the Tests Offered Us in Life – 42:6–28

Since Joseph was not only the "governor of the land" of Egypt, he also was the official who sold the grain (v. 6). This double identification accords well with Joseph's two earlier dreams. In one, the sun, moon, and eleven stars bowed before him (in his position of authority); in the other, his brothers' sheaves bowed before his (in his position of provider). Instantly upon seeing the ten men, Joseph "recognized" his brothers, but he sensed they did not recognize him. This is because some 22 years had passed, and he was almost 40 years of age now, so Joseph chose not to reveal himself immediately to his brothers. Anyway, Joseph now was clean-shaven with a hairstyle that both reflected the Egyptian culture and was clothed in the royal garb of Egyptian administrators. Instead, Joseph decided to speak sternly to his brothers as he inquired where they had come from. They responded, "From the land of Canaan, to buy food" (v. 7).

Joseph must have experienced a rush of emotions and a host of new questions as his brothers now stood before him. What were their attitudes toward him now? Had they had any change of heart in all these years that had transpired since the dastardly deed? How was their father? What about his younger brother, who also was one of Rachel's two children and Joseph's closest full brother?

Joseph seems to have forced himself to exhibit the persona of a hard master as he declared, "You are spies! You have come to detect the weakness of the land" (v. 9). The boys firmly denied this. They depicted themselves as "sons of one man," "honest men" who had merely come to buy food (vv. 10–11). They even went further: "Your servants are twelve … The youngest is now with our father, and one is no more" (v. 13).

Joseph outwardly refused to accept their story, for he still accused all of them of being spies (v. 14). In fact, he said there was a way to test them: "As surely as Pharaoh lives, you will not leave this place unless your youngest brother comes here!" (v. 15). Joseph ordered that one of the ten men go back to Canaan and bring this alleged younger brother while the other nine men would be confined in a guardhouse (vv. 16–17). Joseph must have understood, from their talk amongst themselves in Hebrew, that this would present a monumental challenge!

Regardless, this new demand must have hit the brothers like a ton of bricks! Joseph had hit the very-delicate sore spot in this family. Thus, for the moment they were not worried about their situation; rather, the question was this: How in the world were they going to be able to get permission from their father to let Benjamin come with them to Egypt? Jacob was dead set against such it.

Joseph did speak harshly with them, but not to retaliate against them for how they had treated him years ago; instead, it seems, he wanted to know what was going on in their hearts and minds. They were even more shocked when Joseph asked them if their father was still living and if they had another brother. Moreover, given the fast pace at which all this was happening, Joseph needed time to think. All of this had fallen on him so suddenly; he needed to take counsel with his own feelings and attitudes.

Notice, however, that during this time, apparently, nothing was said about God. Did this say something about the state of the brothers' spirituality all during this time? How can mortals continue to be unreconciled to each other without first being reconciled to God if they wish to enjoy peace and harmony with each other?

Finally, on the third day Joseph had a change of heart, for he urged them: "Do this, and you shall live, for I fear God" (v. 18; the first part of this quote appears in Deuteronomy 6:4; Leviticus 18:5; Luke 10:28b). Joseph taught that proper actions produce proper results, for God's word remains reliable! Thus, the introduction of the fear of God introduced the real dimension of their crime long ago!

The brothers would all be released, except one would be detained in Joseph's custody while the rest returned home for their hungry households (v. 19). But he strictly warned them to bring back this alleged brother if they wanted to purchase any more grain and free the brother who was being held hostage; until they provided such necessary proof, they faced starvation as a family. What could they do except to consent to these terms (v. 20)?

We cannot know for sure whether it had been Joseph's plan, by this line of questioning and harsh words, to bring on them an awakening of their consciences. Suddenly, the brothers started to believe there was a connection between what was taking place in their lives and what they had done to Joseph 22 years ago. The brothers said to one another,

> "Alas, we are being punished on account of our brother: We saw
> the distress of his soul when he besought us, and we would not
> hear. This is why this distress has overtaken us." (v. 21)

Reuben joined in with an admonishment: "Did not I say to you, 'Do not harm the lad,' and you would not listen? Now comes the reckoning for his blood" (v. 22). But what none of them knew was that Joseph understood all that was said, for he did not need an interpreter to help him interpret since his brothers spoke in his own native Hebrew tongue (v. 23) In fact, he was so stirred by this conversation between the brothers that he turned away and wept. After taking some time to recover, he had Simeon taken from the ten men and placed in fetters right in front of their eyes to be imprisoned while the brothers went to bring Benjamin to this Egyptian official.

Apparently, the hearts of the brothers had softened somewhat, as they spoke openly of something they probably had hardly brought up in almost a quarter-century! It would have been interesting also to have a record of the conversation that occurred on the way home from Egypt after this can of worms had been opened! Had the brothers been sorry for what they had done in the past, or were they merely sorry their sin had found them out and had caught up with them?

Joseph ordered that each man should get the measure of grain they came for as well as have their money returned in each sack. Thus, the brothers loaded up their donkeys and went on their way (vv. 25–26). When they stopped that night, one of the men open his sack to feed his donkey, when he discovered his silver had been returned to him (v. 27). When he yelled in surprise about this discovery to his brothers, "their hearts stopped" as they all came up with the same question: "What is this that God has done to us?" (v. 28). Did this remind the brothers of the money they received from the sale of Joseph? They attributed this new dilemma to God—not because he reached down from heaven and put the money in the sack, but because he was now treating them this way because of all they had done to their brother.

Through the Signs or Omens That God Gives Us Through Life – 42:29–38

When the brothers returned to their home in Canaan, they had quite a story to tell their father (vv. 29–35). They said the man in charge of the grain in Egypt spoke harshly and accused them of spying on the land. They were placed in custody for three days, and Simeon was still in jail there. The brothers also explained that if they wanted any more grain, they had to return with Benjamin. Moreover, as they were emptying their sacks, they found that once again the silver they had used to pay for the grain had been returned to each man's sack. This struck a further note of fear in the hearts of these brothers.

As might be expected, Jacob did not welcome all this news easily. Instead, he poured out his heart, saying,

> You have deprived me of my children.
> Joseph is no more
> and [now] Simeon is no more,
> and now you want to take Benjamin.
> Everything is against me! (42:36)

Jacob was adamant: "My son will not go down with you; his brother is dead and he [Benjamin] is the only one left" (38). Reuben tried his best to intervene by pledging his two sons if anything happened to Benjamin on the projected trip to Egypt, but Jacob wasn't buying any of that!

Conclusions

1. Genuine repentance requires not only godly sorrow for sinning against God (contrition), but real faith in the fact that God in his mercy really forgives and forgets our sin.

2. It is easy to just say we forgive another person, but it is harder to really forgive when we come face-to-face with the one(s) who caused the tragedy.

3. God sometimes uses dreams to communicate his plan and will for our loves. But once he has spoken the contents of that dream, we can be sure he will also fulfill it just as certainly.

4. When God wants to bring a revival to any people or nation, 2 Chronicles 7:14 teaches that if God's people who are called by his name will humble themselves, seek his face, pray, and turn from their wicked ways, then God will forgive their sin and heal their land/nation.

Joseph's Brothers Return to Egypt with Benjamin
Genesis 43:1–34

Naturally, there seemed to be no discussion for a time over Joseph's ultimatum that the brothers must bring Benjamin to Egypt if they wanted any more grain. In the meantime, poor Simeon was biding his time in the house of bondage. But the famine's persistence would not allow Jacob's family the luxury of postponing this discussion much longer. In fact, it was Jacob himself who raised the issue when the supply of grain the brothers had brought back was exhausted; he urged, "Go back and buy us a little more food" (43:2). But the real elephant in the room was his steadfast refusal to allow Benjamin to return with the boys to Egypt. Meanwhile the famine throughout the whole region remained "intense" (Hebrew *kabed*, v. 1).

This time, the fourth son in the line of twelve stepped forward instead of Reuben as the spokesperson for the others (v. 3). Reuben had said he would put the lives of his two sons on the line if anything happened to Benjamin in Egypt (42:37). But Judah said Jacob could personally hold him responsible if anything happened to his favorite son. Moreover, as if Jacob had forgotten the stringent terms set by the Egyptian in charge of the grain, he carefully reminded Jacob what that man had told them: "The man adamantly warned us, 'You shall not appear before me unless your brother is with you'" (v. 3). Then, as if to emphasize his point, Judah announced, "If you do not send our brother with us, we will not go down'" (v. 5a). It's not clear whether Judah embellished Joseph's words or just gave a loose paraphrase, but he "quoted" more to his father than what Scripture records of Joseph's actual speech.

Suddenly in v. 6 the narrator referred to Jacob as "Israel." Why the sudden switch? Some commentators think verses 6, 8, and 11, which use "Israel," were deliberately changed later on, but they give no rationale. Another commentator suggested "Jacob" referred to the father's suffering and human side of his person, while "Israel" underscored the dignity and office of the patriarch. Perhaps! But we do not know with any certainty.

The brothers continued to volunteer other questions that the man in Egypt supposedly inquired of them, but Jacob was not impressed. He asked, "Why have you hurt me so badly as to tell the man that you had a brother?" (v. 6b). Jacob's point seemed to be that even speaking true things can be unwise if it might serve no good purpose.

It was finally left for Judah to force the issue with the reality they faced: "Then Judah urged Israel his father: 'Let the lad go with me, that we may be off and on our way if any of us is to live and not die—we, and you, and our little ones'" (v. 8). Judah didn't refer to Benjamin by name, but it was obvious that if they didn't soon go and get some food for the family, Benjamin too would soon die anyway. One way of the other, they were facing death no matter how you pictured the situation!

Judah referred to Benjamin as "the lad," but he was just a few years younger than Joseph. Thus, what may have qualified Benjamin as a *na`ar* (Hebrew for a "lad") was his unmarried status, not his specific age. Judah wanted to get going, for with all this arguing and stalling, they could have gone to Egypt and been there and back twice by now (v. 10). Judah pledged to act as surety for the young man. Finally, with that argument, the deadlock was broken.

Israel Gives Permission for the Brothers to Take Benjamin to Egypt – 43:11–14

We may have here an explanation for the switch from "Jacob" to "Israel." The narrative picks up where it left off; it is one that continues to carry out God's plan for his people and for the nations of the world. Therefore, it was not Reuben's persuasiveness (his argument did not impress Jacob), nor Judah's arguments, that moved Jacob (now called "Israel") or God to act. God who was the One who surely inclined Israel's heart to follow his plan, for "the steps of a good man are ordered by the Lord." Israel the patriarch was willing finally to trust the Lord who had blessed him in so many other ways. And even though he trusted in the Lord, Israel still thought it prudent to give such gifts as might ingratiate himself and his boys to the much-talked-about man in Egypt!

Therefore, Israel instructed his sons to take some of the best fruits from the land of Canaan as a present—a little balm, a little honey, spices, myrrh, nuts and almonds (almost the same items the Ishmaelites were carrying to sell in Egypt, 37:25b). It is worth noting that even in the years of famine over the whole Near East, Canaan still produced some rare commodities not found in Egypt.

Their father Israel seemed satisfied that this was how things must finally be, regardless of what may happen (v. 11). So, Israel sent the eleven men off with this blessing: "May God Almighty (literally "El-Shaddai," Gen. 17:1; 28:3; 35:11; 49:25; Exodus 6:3) grant you mercy before the man so that he will let your other brother and Benjamin come back with you. As for me, if I am bereaved, I am bereaved" (v. 14). This is similar to Esther's much-later pronouncement: "If I perish, I perish" (Esther 4:16). Israel's benediction on the brothers was repeated in the events that followed as seen, for example, in Joseph's being "deeply moved" (Hebrew *rahamayw*, "his mercy") upon seeing Benjamin. Moreover, in each of the passages where "El-Shaddai" is used, God is the Lord who blesses and makes promises and keeps covenants. Israel's prayer was that El-Shaddai would "be merciful" in bringing them back to Canaan again.

God Gives Permission for the Brothers' Sack to Contain Treasure – 43:15–25

When Joseph saw that Benjamin was with them (v. 16), as the men seem to have been waiting outside Joseph's house for him to arrive, for he had instructed his steward to take the men to his home. Then the steward was to prepare a feast, and the man second-in-command of all Egypt would dine with the eleven at noon (v. 16b). But this only made the men all the more apprehensive, for they presumed the whole thing was a setup so that this Egyptian ruler could eventually overpower them, force them into slavery and take their donkeys from them as well (v. 18).

Apparently, all of them approached the steward together as one and began to explain, as if in a chorus, that they had come to Egypt only to purchase grain (vv. 19–20). "But when we opened our sacks, there was the silver right on top of the grain. That is why we have brought back double the price of the grain, so you would not think we had stolen it" (vv. 21–22).

The steward must have been in on the trick Joseph was playing on his brothers, for he quickly and easily replied, "It's all right (or "rest assured"). Don't be afraid. Your God, the God of your father, has given you treasure (Hebrew *matmon*, "hidden treasure") in your sacks. I received your silver" (v. 23). The steward called it a "buried treasure," for the Hebrew word is made up of the verb *taman*, "to hide, to bury." but he did not infer that the man had to dig for it, for that treasure was in the "mouth" of their sacks. However, God used the steward to remind us of one of the central themes of Genesis: "the God of your fathers has given you treasure" by blessing you (v. 23b).

The issue of their being spies does not come up again, for after all, they had returned with Benjamin, so that charge was dead. (And we know the "charge" of spying was simply used by Joseph to test the men and their feelings for the brother they had sold years ago.) But why were they being entertained so lavishly and so expensively by the second-most-powerful man in all Egypt? Since they were in a famine, perhaps it had been a long time since the men had seen such a sumptuous meal set before them.

God Gives Permission for Benjamin to Meet Joseph – 43:26–34

When Joseph arrived at his house, the eleven men had the gifts they had brought already laid out for him (v. 26). However, Joseph made no recorded comments on the gifts from Canaan, instead focusing immediately on a greater concern: "How is your aged father? … Is he still living?" (v. 27). The men replied, "He is still alive and well" (v. 28). Joseph may well have been worried that he might never see his father alive again.

As Joseph looked around, he suddenly caught a glance of his mother's son Benjamin. "Is this your younger brother, the one you told me about? … God be gracious to you, my son" (v. 29). Twenty-three years before was the last time he had seen Benjamin, when he was still a toddler. All of this was too much for Joseph, and he could not maintain his emotions, so he quickly retreated to a private room to weep. He had been "deeply moved by the sight of his brother" (v. 30).

After Joseph had regained his composure and washed his face, he returned and ordered the food be served. Joseph sat by himself, as did the Egyptians, for that was the custom of that culture. The men were amazed to notice that each one of them had been seated in their birth-order. But even more humorous was the fact that "Benjamin's portion was five times as much as anyone else's" (vv. 33–34). So, the men feasted with the Egyptians and for the moment drank freely with the man of Egypt.

It is surprising that the eleven men had not yet figured out what was going on. They seemed to have no inkling of an idea who Joseph was. But how did Joseph know how to arrange them around the table in their chronological birth-order? They had not shared that information with him. And why did he make Benjamin the person who was honored with five times the portions they all received? Were the brothers altogether obtuse?

But Joseph wanted to know if his brothers had changed over the past quarter-century. Or had they merely transferred their hatred for Joseph to his brother Benjamin? Surely Joseph's ears were sharply tuned to pick up any bits of information while the brothers talked among themselves. He had to put them to one more final test to answer these dangling questions in his mind. Joseph would learn what the attitudes of the ten men were toward their father and their youngest brother.

Conclusions

1. God can and does use physical famines to call his people to search their hearts about any unresolved sin in their lives.

2. God changed their father's name from "Jacob" to "Israel," for the Lord was continuing to bring a blessing as he promised to his people and as that name signified.

3. Israel (Jacob) emphasized God's watch-care and faithfulness using the name "El-Shaddai" for God, meaning the One who nourishes.

4. Joseph's steward taught the men an important truth: The Lord their God was the One who had put hidden treasure in their sacks, so be thankful to him and bless his name!

Joseph's Cup in Benjamin's Sack

Genesis 44:1–34

Soon after the brothers had finished eating their meal at Joseph's home, Joseph ordered his steward to fill the eleven brothers' sacks with grain and for the second time to return the silver they had paid for the grain back in the tops of the men's sacks. But the restored payment from the brothers is not mentioned again in this chapter. Instead, a much more serious charge is made against the men: They have stolen Joseph's silver cup. This was arranged by Joseph so Benjamin would be the victim this time. Had this silver cup been prominently displayed where they had dined, or had it just been purposely displayed so the guests could examine it? This cup or goblet (Hebrew *gabia*), in Jeremiah 35, was a common pitcher of about 8 or 10 inches high for holding either wine or water, but here in Gen. 44 and Exodus 25, 37, it is a "cup," not a pitcher. So, what was Joseph up to? What was he trying to find out by setting up this whole scenario of hiding his cup in Benjamin's sack? Let us look at the text more carefully to deduce what is going on here.

The Charge: Benjamin Is Accused of Stealing Joseph's Cup – 44:1–14

It is clear that Joseph had deliberately set up a scheme, through his steward, so that his special cup would be found in his younger brother's sack. Joseph wanted to see if his brothers would abandon Benjamin just as they had so brazenly put him up for sale to the

Ishmaelites. This test, then, would be greater than all of prior tests the second-highest official in the land had used.

After the men had feasted with this official the previous day, they gathered their sacks as the morning-light dawned. They loaded the sacks on their donkeys as they set off to return home (44:3). So far, things had gone much better than the men could have expected. Simeon had been released from his confinement in prison, where he had awaited his brothers' return; they had been treated rather royally in the invitation to dine with the second-greatest man in Egypt, and Benjamin had survived the ordeal and was now with them on their way back to Canaan. Why had they worried so much over nothing? It was all turning out very nicely!

But they had not traveled very far when suddenly Joseph's steward caught up with the small party of brothers and charged them with stealing from the man in Egypt who issued out the amounts of grain each was to get (v. 4). When the steward caught up with the eleven men bound for Canaan (v. 6), his charge against them was simply outrageous: "Why have you repaid good with evil? Isn't this the cup my master drinks from and also uses for divination [in your possession]?" (vv. 4b–5).

The brothers' reply was weak, to say the least, for all that they could muster was, "Why does my lord say such things? Far be it from your servants to do anything like that!" (v. 7). To strengthen their case for righteousness, they mentioned they had indeed brought back the doubled amount of silver that had perhaps been mistakenly placed in their sacks when they made their first trip to Egypt (v. 8). Moreover, to show how sure they were that none had done such a dastardly deed, they uttered an oath that if any of the eleven were guilty of such a crime, that brother would die, and the rest would become servants of the steward's boss (v. 9).

So, the steward began to canvass all eleven grain sacks, starting with the oldest sons. The sacks were opened one after another without any cup—until they came to the last one, Benjamin's sack (v. 11). There they found the stolen silver cup. The men were shocked and deeply grieved, but without any credible explanation as they tore their garments in deep consternation and torment.

But what was this "cup of divination" all about? Divination is the practice of attempting to use supernatural means to gain knowledge of the future or of unknown things. Divination and magic are known from the early days of Bible times. The Gentile prophet Balaam found the methods of divination were powerless against the people of Israel, whom God had already blessed (Numbers 23:23, 24:1). Laban, Jacob's uncle, claimed to have superior knowledge as a result of divination (Gen. 39:27).

Had this "cup" been used for "divination," by pouring oil on top of a cup of water or vice-versa (called "oleomancy" and "hydromancy," respectively) to observe how the liquids formed kinds of images (Gen. 44:1–5, 15). But Joseph was given the ability to interpret dreams (37:5–11; 40:5–19), so his wisdom came from a revelation from God, not a duplication of pagan techniques. The cup may have carried this title due to its prior royal usage, but nowhere in the narrative did Joseph resort to any of the methods associated with such cups in the surrounding culture. Joseph's referring to the cup as a vessel for divination was likely just a ruse to heighten its importance.

In the meantime, Joseph had not left his house, for he knew the men would be returning soon, as he had set the trap for them (v. 14). This was turning out to be one of the most tragic days these men of Canaan had ever lived. How had it all happened? Who or what was against them? Was this all linked somehow to their murky past? What should or could the brothers do? It appeared they had been caught red-handed as thieves by the steward. Who would ever have guessed that Benjamin had this character fault? Should they try to save him, or let him get what he deserved?

The Response: Judah's Acceptance of All Blame and Guilt – 44:15–34

The eleven brothers solemnly trooped into Joseph's house once again as Joseph began lecturing them, "What is this you have done? Don't you know that a man like me can find things out by divination?" (v. 15). Was Joseph suddenly enjoying this for the moment?

"Come on, Joseph," we readers plead. "Have a heart! You know they're innocent. What's the point of this charade? Are you trying to get a read on whether the brothers have had a change in their hearts and whether there is any evidence of a character change with any signs of loving kindness and mercy about them now, compared to those former days?"

What has otherwise seemed to be Joseph exacting slow revenge on his brothers for the rotten deal they dealt him long ago can now be seen for what it really is. Joseph's purpose was not revenge but repentance. Throughout these schemes, the brothers were coming to an awareness of their guilt and a readiness to acknowledge it. Of course, the issue of the cup was the most pressing issue on their minds, but within the compass of the whole narrative about Joseph, the words take on the scope of a confession of their long-standing guilt over what they had done to him!

Judah stepped forward. From here on out he will emerge as the new leader who will replace Reuben in his former position as the "firstborn" one. Judah made no excuse or rationalization for what had happened; he made no attempts to smooth over the guilt or sinful actions of the brothers with regard to any cup. Instead, he chose these words as his reply: "What can we say? … God has uncovered your servants' guilt. We are now my lord's slaves—we ourselves and the one who was found to have the cup" (v. 16).

Was Judah also acknowledging anything related to the ten brothers' previous sin against Joseph? Judah did not mention Joseph's name, but since he could not define or explain why all this was happening to them, he knew God had seen what they had done to their brother, and thus there was no other explanation for their misfortunes except that God was calling for a day of reckoning from them because they sold their brother. They were not guilty of the present calamities they had been thrust into, but they sure were guilty of that long-ago act. In Judah's mind and theology, they were not guilty of stealing a cup, but they were certainly guilty of a far greater sin, the selling and planned murder of their brother. And that is what God had uncovered about them in all the recent troubles that had been sent to them! Behind all they were experiencing, God's sovereign hand was clearly evident!

Wow! What must Joseph have sensed and felt in the moment of Judah's speech? Wasn't this what he had been looking for? Didn't this show real sorrow and confession of the brothers' sins? Wasn't it time to stop the charades and level with his brothers about who it was they were talking to? We want Joseph now to show some compassion!

Not yet, for it seems there still was one more area Joseph wanted to investigate first. How did the brothers truly feel about their aged father? Would they respect and honor him, or was he so partial to Rebekah's sons (in their estimation) that there would be no peace in that home? Joseph declined Judah's offer to incarcerate all eleven of the brothers; he would enslave only Benjamin, the one in whose sack the cup was found (v. 17). This would reveal to Joseph whether these men had any real concern for their aged father and what impact this would have on him.

Judah's response evidenced a real change and a profound advancement from the cold, calculated speech he had given almost a quarter-century ago as the brothers were selling Joseph as a slave (37:26ff). Previously, he had spoken out of envy, spite, and a heart filed with anger because of Joseph's irritating way of pushing himself forward and as the hero of his dreams.

Judah, in his appeal to Joseph, repeats the previous conversations so many times in retelling past events that only four of the fifteen verses (vv. 18–32) are without any direct quote from the prior discourses. Judah quotes Joseph addressing his brothers three times (vv. 19, 21, 23). He uses the word "servant(s)" ten times. Judah also is either very careful in recognizing Joseph's high station by calling him "my lord" six times (vv. 18, 19, 20, 22, 24), or he is deliberately spreading Joseph's honor on thick to gain favor. Judah also refers to his "father" fifteen times.

Of course, Judah knows not everything of this retold story is accurate when he quotes his father to Joseph, but given his situation, there was no other way to tell the story. For example, a wild animal hadn't killed Joseph, as Judah cites Jacob as saying; the brothers sold him into slavery, then killed a goat and sprinkled its blood on his coat.

One wonders if the men ever thought twice about Joseph's dreams on their trip to Egypt. What if they ran into him again? That might have made them a little more cognizant of what might be going on in the midst of all their drama.

Judah's appeal to Joseph was this: "If the boy is not with us when I go back home to your servant my father, and if my father, whose life is closely bound up with the boy's life, sees that the boy isn't there, he will die" (v. 30). Judah concluded: "Now then, please let your servant remain here as my lord's slave in place of the boy, and let the boy return with his brothers. How can I go back to my father if the boy is not with me? No! Do not let me see the misery that would come on my father" (vv. 33–34). While Judah was concerned for his father's health, it is also clear that he thought the only way out of the quandary the brothers had somehow gotten themselves into was for him to become a slave in Benjamin's place.

Conclusions

1. In the second visit to Egypt, there was a growing consciousness of the guilt the brothers had been silently nursing for almost a quarter of a century, and Judah became the spokesman for the group to that effect.

2. Joseph deliberately targeted his younger brother Benjamin by having the cup of divination placed in Benjamin's sack, for he knew how sensitive this issue was for their father Jacob.

3. Joseph showed no affinity for or use of any forms of divination to gain knowledge of the future. Why resort to pagan resources when he had access to the revelation of God not only for his own dreams but for those of others as well.

4. Although Judah could not explain why the brothers were suffering so much in almost every move they made in Egypt, in his words, they knew God was uncovering their guilt and unconfessed sin.

5. Judah, who had engineered the plan to get rid of Joseph, became the man who would volunteer to take Benjamin's place as a slave.

Lesson 8

Joseph Reveals His Identity to His Brothers

Genesis 45:1–24

Finally, the climax the reader has been waiting for came in an outburst from the second-highest official in Egypt. That man "could no longer control himself before all his attendants," so he cried out, "Have everyone leave my presence" (45:1). This must have at first confused the brothers, for they had been accused of stealing Joseph's divining cup. Judah was pleading for mercy. For the men from Canaan, such an outburst from the man who was interrogating them may have seemed to indicate they were in serious trouble. Perhaps they had so angered Joseph that he was going to imprison all of them right away! This chief of Egypt's food-distribution services had always addressed them sternly. But with this outburst, there was no way this whole affair was going to end positively. In fact, you can almost feel the brothers shudder and grimace as the head man in Egypt let loose with an emotional outburst that could be heard all over the place!

After the man in charge had dismissed all of the Egyptian staff, Joseph was left in his Egyptian home alone with his eleven brothers. With that outburst came a rush of tears and bitter mourning and sobbing that grew so loud that the Egyptians nearby and those in Pharaoh's household knew something strange was going on, but they did not have a clue as to what it was. This is the third time the narrative records that Joseph was weeping (42:24, 43:30, 45:2). But why? What was the matter with him?

Joseph Reveals Himself to His Brothers – 45:1–7

"I am Joseph." With just two words, *ʿani yosep*, Joseph let out the secret he had been holding back on (v. 3). He followed that with a question he had previously asked and already knew the answer to, but as if to fill the vacuum of the brothers' stunned silence, he asked again: "Is my father still living?" (Recall that previously he had said "*your* father.") That announcement must have struck his brothers like a ton of bricks, adding to their utter confusion and fear, for not one of them dared utter a peep after that startling disclosure. You can imagine them thinking, *Did I hear that correctly? Did he say he was Joseph?* Suddenly terror struck the men. What on earth was going to happen now? They were totally unprepared for what they were hearing! They were just plain terrified! In addition to that declaration, Joseph added a damning clause: "your brother whom you sold into Egypt" (v. 4). Only Joseph and his brothers would have known that, so was it really him? Moreover, he was addressing them in his native tongue of Hebrew instead of speaking through an interpreter. How did he know Hebrew?

Instead of continuing to talk, Joseph urged the men to come close to him. Wow! This was the brother they probably had not dared to talk openly about for decades, and here he had said, "I am your brother Joseph!" *This is impossible! It can't be happening, can it?*

But while they were trying to get the idea of his presence straight in their confused minds, suddenly they Joseph gave them a reality-check on a topic they had never thought much about before. He said, "Do not be distressed, and do not be angry with yourselves for selling me here, because it was to save lives that God sent me ahead of you" (v. 5). Perhaps what suddenly played back in their minds was what they had regarded as those stupid dreams the ten brothers hated so much. Had Joseph truly become the ruler over the whole land of Egypt? And had they bowed down before him, as he once said he dreamt? Impossible! This was not happening! Wow!

Up to this point, only two years of the famine had taken place, but there were "five more years" to come, during which there would be "neither plowing nor harvesting" (v. 6). All forms of agriculture would cease.

As with TV shows, it is time for a "commercial break" so we the readers can catch our breath.

Excursus: The Egyptian Story of the "Tale of the Two Brothers"

We pause to investigate the Papyrus D'Orbiney, an Egyptian text that dates to around 1225 B.C.E. It is a well-told, non-biblical story about two brothers, and it possibly offers some striking similarities to the narrative about Joseph.

In this fictional Egyptian tale, Bata lived with his older brother Anubis, whom he served faithfully in his house and fields. One day, Anubis' wife tried to seduce Bata, much as Potiphar's wife tried to seduce Joseph. When Bata rejected her advances, as Joseph rejected Potiphar's wife's attempt to get him to sleep with her, she outright lied to her husband Anubis just as Potiphar's wife lied to her husband about Joseph. So enraged was Anubis on hearing his wife's story about his brother's attempted rape of his wife, he decided to kill him. He tried to do so by hiding behind the barn door as Bata drove the cows into the barn for the night. But the cows warned him that Anubis was lurking behind the door, so Bata fled. A lake filled with crocodiles magically appeared to separate the boys, and Anubis returned home and proceeded to kill his wife instead!

Meanwhile, Bata cut out his heart and placed it high up in a pine tree he had planted, presumably rendering him immortal. The gods graciously fashioned a beautiful wife for Bata. But when she, as an immortal woman, entered Pharaoh's harem, and revealed the secret that Bata could be killed by cutting down the pine tree with his heart high up in it, things grew mighty dangerous for him. The tree was felled, as she had urged. Anubis, who by now had been reconciled to Bata, found his brother's heart from the downed tree and restored Bata to life again.

Bata transformed himself into a bull and carried Anubis into Pharaoh's court, where Bata's estranged wife became alarmed and persuaded Pharaoh to sacrifice the bull. Bata's blood caused two trees to sprout. Now his beautiful new wife, realizing Bata was still alive, arranged to have the trees cut down, but a splinter flew into her mouth, and she became pregnant. She bore a son, whom Pharaoh raised as his very own crown prince. The boy she bore turned out to be no one less than Bata himself, so in due course of events he, Bata, became Pharaoh and he appointed Anubis his viceroy. I guess they lived happily ever after!

Of course, the story is rather outlandish by all decent standards of reality, but it does exhibit some rather interesting parallels to the Joseph narrative. If the Egyptian Papyrus D'Orbiney was not the earliest iteration of this story, and it actually was written for the first time earlier than 1225 B.C.E., then despite its bizarre quality, it may reflect some remnants of a factual sort and reflect a tone or two that accords with the Joseph narrative. However, if this Egyptian tale came after the time of Joseph, then this tale may have been influenced by a few aspects of the biblical narrative.

Joseph Teaches His Brothers the Providence of God – 45:8

Joseph clearly stressed to his brothers that it was not they who sent him to Egypt but God himself. Joseph did not flaunt the high position he had attained, nor any of his achievements; it was God who had been behind all the things that had happened to him over the last 22 years. To back up what he had just declared, Joseph gave his three titles: "father to Pharaoh, lord of his entire household, and ruler of all Egypt" (v. 8).

Where in Joseph's pilgrimage these past 22 years had he gained this viewpoint and attitude on his suffering and theological explanation for his letdowns? Surely when he saw his brothers bowing down to him, he must have recalled parts of his dreams. But had any of this explanation have come together for him earlier than that? Why then do we never hear even a murmur of complaint from Joseph in all those years? Was he so sure of God's purpose that he waited patiently for providence to work on his behalf? Possibly!

Joseph's Message for Jacob – 45:9–15

Joseph had a message for his brothers to deliver to their father. It was an urgent word for his brothers to hasten his invitation to Jacob to come to Egypt; a word from a son formerly believed dead; the actual message itself; and an encouragement not to delay (v. 9). Joseph put at the head of his message that what had happened to him was all about God, for "God has made me lord of all Egypt" (v. 9d). There would be a place for the whole family to live in the Goshen region of Egypt. Jacob was to come with all his children, grandchildren, flocks, and herds—indeed, with all he had. Joseph would provide for the family's well-being, for there were still five more years of famine ahead. If they did not come, they and all their household would become destitute (v. 11).

Joseph now referred to Jacob as "my father" (v. 9a) as he had in v. 3, instead of "our father." But he still referred to the eleven men as "your sons" rather than "my brothers," possibly showing more of an intimacy to his father, but a little bit of a distance from his ten brothers.

Having cared for first things first, Joseph now turned to his brothers, whose heads must have still been spinning! He had urged the men to "go up" immediately and "come [back] down" as soon as possible (v. 9). No doubt the brothers wanted Joseph to stop and tell them how he had managed to land such a good job! They possibly wanted to know what had taken place after the Ishmaelites carried him away on their camels. Did he go directly to Pharaoh's palace to live? Did he get additional schooling from the palace? Questions like that must have sailed through their minds, but particularly distressing would have been, *How are we going to tell our father that you are still alive? He thinks you are dead! Do we have to tell him how this came about by our doings?* Joseph must have helped the men to refocus, for he said, "Tell my father about all the honor accorded me in Egypt and about everything you have seen" (v. 13).

But no more talk for the moment, Joseph urged, as he threw his arms around his brother Benjamin, and then around each of his brothers as he affectionately kissed each one and wept over them (vv. 14–15).

Pharaoh Confirms Joseph's Invitation to the Family – 45:16–20

The report that Joseph's brothers had come to Egypt for grain spread throughout Pharaoh's palace (v. 16). This pleased Pharaoh and his courtiers. Pharaoh himself added to the instructions Joseph had given: They were to load their animals, go to Canaan, and return to Egypt. "Bring your father and your families back to me," he said. "I will assign to you the best of the land of Egypt and you can enjoy the fat of the land" (vv. 17–19).

Excursus: The Flooded Land and Bahr Yussef

Pharaoh did not mention Goshen, as Joseph had, as the land that would be made available for them. Goshen was part of the eastern delta of the Nile River known today as el-Sharkia Governorate ("Eastern Province"). The Bible describes Goshen as being on the eastern border of Egypt (Gen. 46:28, 29; Exodus 13:17). The clue that Goshen is best identified with the eastern district of the delta is seen in the modern name of one of its major towns, Fakus. The site of Avaris/Ramesses is just north of Fakus.

Archaeologist David Rohl makes an observation most interpreters of the Joseph narrative usually miss: In Joseph's dream, the seven good cows came up out of the Nile River, as did the seven ugly cows. It is associated with the seven years of plenty and the seven years of famine. But Rohl connects the famine not to seven years of drought but of extensive flooding over the land—perhaps four to five times the normal water level of the Nile. Thus, the Nile River, which has its sources in central Africa and the Ethiopian Highlands, sent water downstream and as it often flooded the Nile. But in this case, for seven years the Nile flooded at just the right level, which is about 30 feet above the year-round average at the first cataract in Elephantine.

But what would happen if there was a climactic shift in the weather patterns changed that water level? Rohl asked, "What [would] happen if the tropical zone around the equator [from which the water descended to Egypt] ... shifted northwards, causing rain to fall more heavily on the Ethiopian Highlands?"[1] "What that would do is to push the dry Saharan climate into the land of Israel, into the area where Jacob and his family [were] living ... while the Egyptians were suffering high floods at the same time."[2]

---

1. Timothy P. Mahoney, *Patterns of Evidence – The Exodus,* St Louis Park, MN, Thinking Man Media, pp. 130 – 31.
2. Ibid., p. 130

Moreover, on the southern border of Egypt is a remarkable feature at a place where the water comes through a gorge. On the cliff face are inscriptions marking the height of the Nile, which shows there were levels four times higher than normal at the time of the Pharaoh Amenemhat III, dated around 1850 B.C.E., which is approximately the time of Joseph!

There is also something else that connects Joseph to this flooding in Egypt: a canal or waterway that flows parallel to the Nile and empties into a large lake called the "Fayum." It is located in the Sahara Desert on the east side of the Nile, with a canal feeding it from run-off water from the Nile River called "Bahr Yussef," meaning "the waterway of Joseph," constructed in the 12th Dynasty of Egypt's Middle Kingdom. "Bahr Yussef" is Arabic, though it was built around the time of Amenemhat III, which is the time of Joseph.

All of this coincides with the development of the city of Avaris, a Middle Egyptian Kingdom of the 13th Dynasty. Excavated by Manfred Bietak, Avaris is just underneath the city of Ramesses. Hence the name of Ramesses in the Bible is anachronistic, meaning the reference is a modern marker for the same location that came some 100 or more years before the building of Ramesses. But the people who dwelt in Avaris had Syrian and Asiatic roots, meaning they were Hebrews!

For example, we see a Syria house the Austrian archaeological excavators called *Mittelsaal* ("middle-room house") in the heart of Avaris. This is the type of house Abraham came from up north during the Middle Bronze Age and one you would expect Jacob to build if he lived here. This suggests the early Israelites may have lived here. But this house was flattened, and a palace was built on top of it with courtyards, colonnades, and audience chambers. Even more interesting, in the garden behind this palace, archaeologists found 12 main graves with memorial chapels on top. And one had a pyramid tomb, which in Egypt was reserved for pharaohs and queens. Inside the chapel of this special tomb was a statue of a man with red hair, pale yellow skin, and a throw-stick, like a boomerang, and on the back of his shoulder were the faintest vestiges of colored stripes of perhaps a multicolored coat.

Joseph Sends His Brothers to Tell Jacob to Come to Egypt – 45:21–28

So, the brothers have finally learned that Joseph was still alive, and all their families were being welcomed to live in Egypt. Pharaoh approved of Joseph's plan and loaned him some Egyptian U-Haul trailers to cart back on these wagons the new clothes Joseph had given them, along with provisions for the journey (v. 19).

Joseph received five changes of clothing and 300 pieces of silver (v. 22), but to each of the other brothers Joseph gave one change of clothes only. He added some gifts for Jacob, including ten donkeys loaded with some of Egypt's finest products and ten she-asses loaded with corn, bread, and such provisions as his father might need for the trip to Egypt (v. 23).

Joseph instructed his brothers, "Don't quarrel on the way!" (v. 24). Thus, the group left for Canaan. But when they reached home, they made the surprising statement that "Joseph is still living and is ruler over the entire land of Egypt" (v. 26). Jacob turned "numb, for he did not believe them" (v. 26b). However, after they shared all that Joseph had said to them, and when he saw the wagons Pharaoh sent to transport him to Egypt, "his spirit … was revived" (v. 27). "It is enough," Jacob concluded. "My son Joseph is still alive! I must go down and see him before I die" (v. 28).

Conclusions

1. Joseph apparently did not get any joy or pleasure out of deceiving his brothers about who he was, but it was done for a purpose.

2. That Joseph did not immediately reveal himself to his kin furthers the central idea of this whole narrative—God is ultimately the One who is behind all that is happening, and he is working it for our good (50:20). "God sent me ahead of you to save lives" (45:5; see also 42:2, 18; 43:8).

3. The close of the book of Genesis, with Pharaoh twice giving brothers "good" (45:18, 20) and the "best" of the land returns to where Genesis began, with God giving the "good" of the land to Adam.

4. The contrast between Jacob's "numbered heart" (45:26) and his later "revived spirit" is similar to what appears later in Scripture with the contrast between a lack of faith ("numbered heart") and believing faith ("revived heart"). See Psalm 51:10 and Jeremiah 31:33–34.

Lesson 9

Joseph's Father and Family Settle in Egypt

Genesis 46:1–34

Jacob likely still lived in Hebron (35:27, 37:14); it seems that it was from there he set out to journey to Egypt. Now Jacob will soon see the son who for 22 years he had thought dead! He traveled first from Hebron to Beersheba, where he stopped long enough to offer sacrifices to the God of his father Isaac (v. 1). Was his sacrifice an act of thanksgiving to God for giving back to him his son Joseph, or was it just plain thanksgiving for holding to his promise to constantly be with them as the people of promise? Anyway, Beersheba was important to Jacob and his family, for it was at that same spot where God had appeared to Jacob's father Isaac and reminded him that he was none other than the "God of [your] father Abraham" (26:23–25). Isaac built an altar in Beersheba (26:25), and now, a whole generation later, his son stops there to offer a sacrifice to God before he speaks. The fact that the word for "sacrifice," *zabach*, appears only twice in Genesis (see 31:54) is most significant. Since it is preceded by a word from God, this is a good indication that Jacob was giving a spontaneous expression of gratitude to God for the way things had finally turned out and for the fact that the Living God had kept all his promises to Israel!

Jacob Leaves Canaan to Go to Egypt – 46:1–7

Jacob stopped at Beersheba to offer sacrifices in worship to the God of his father Isaac. There God spoke to Jacob one night, just as he had appeared to Abraham in a grand vision years ago (15:5ff) and even at times to foreigners such as Abimelech (20:3) and Laban (31:24). Jacob himself had also experienced such meetings with God on previous nights (28:10ff, 32:21ff).

Just as God had repeated Abraham's name twice when he spoke to him on Mount Moriah (22:11; and in the same way repeated Moses' name in Exodus 3:4, and Samuel's name in 1 Samuel 3:10, or even did the same for Saul, renamed Paul in Acts 9:4), so he repeated Jacob's name on this night as well (46:2). Surprisingly, this text used both names for Joseph's father: "God spoke to Israel in a night vision. He said: 'Jacob, Jacob...'" (46:2). Contrary to what modern liberal exegetes say of this use of dual names for the patriarch, this does *not* indicate the use of two different sources for this narrative. No, it was God's way of reminding Jacob that God had renamed him because he was the heir of the promise-plan. But since it has been some time since God had appeared to Israel at Bethel (35:9ff) at Bethel, could it be that those were years when Jacob's fellowship with God had been diminished? Not necessarily, just as God continued to give his promises all through his life, the Lord made those promises to Abraham in his first meeting with him in 12:1–3, with his final word to him in 22:15–18. Similarly, God gave his first talk to Jacob in 28:13–16 and his last talk in 46:2–4.

God's word to Israel in vv. 3–4 was the same as he had repeated to the other two patriarchs three times previously (15:1, 21:17, 26:24): "Do not be fearful." In fact, God's message had four parts: God's self-identification: "I am the God of your father"; the divine assurance: "Do not be fearful"; the possible object of their fear: i.e., "about going down to Egypt"; and the divine promise: "for into a great nation I will form you there."

Perhaps Jacob was so thrilled over the supreme prospect of seeing his son again that it preempted any ordinary fears he may have had about going down to Egypt. Previously, God had warned Isaac not to go down to Egypt (26:2), but what had been denied to Isaac for other reasons was now being opened up by the Lord for Jacob, for they were now carrying out God's plan for the family the Lord had called and elected for this purpose.

Jacob's journey into Egypt was not that of a visitor's quick trip; he would reside in the land for quite a long time, as the end of v. 3 noted: "for into a great nation I will form you there." The surprising factor is that this formation of Jacob's family as a nation will take place outside of Canaan, even though they are living in another nation altogether, Egypt! Moreover, in addition to Jacob being accompanied by his family, his herds and flocks, and his possessions, God himself would personally escort him (v. 4a). He is told this by a direct revelation from God. But even beyond that assurance of the divine presence, God promised another important feature of this whole move: "I myself will bring you back [to the land of Canaan]" (4b). This was not directed only to Jacob physically and personally, for we know Jacob would leave Egypt in a coffin (50:26). In the three references in v. 4 to "you/your," there is a typical oscillation in Hebrew between the individual Jacob and the collective designation for the community or nation, a kind of "corporate solidarity" of the one and the many!

So, Jacob left Beersheba as his sons carried their father along with the little ones and wives in the wagons Pharaoh had provided to transport them (v. 5). Thus, the whole family, along with their cattle and all their possessions, entered into Egypt (v. 6). Even though we know of only one daughter by name, Dinah, there were other daughters born to Jacob (34:9, 16, 21).

Jacob's Extended Family Listed as Seventy – 46:8–27

Once again, as the text begins to list the names of this family, two names are given to this patriarch: "Israel" and "Jacob" as they were in 46:2, 8. This genealogy has six parts:

1. An introduction – (v. 8a–b),

2. The sons of Leah (vv. 8c–15),

3. The sons by Zilpah (vv. 16–18),

4. The sons by Rachel (vv. 19–22),

5. The sons by Bilhah (vv. 23–25), and

6. A summarizing statement (vv. 26–27).

This gets complicated! Leah contributes 33 descendants to Jacob including six sons, 25 grandsons, and two great-grandsons. Excluding Er and Onan (v. 12), who were put to death in Canaan (38:7, 10), the number is 31. With Dinah the number goes to 32; counting with them Jacob, the number is 33.

Jacob's wives produce twice the number of descendants, i.e., 46 or 47 if Dinah is counted, as the concubines (v. 23). Leah has 32 descendants (33 if Dinah is counted); Rachel has 14, for a total of 46 or 47. Zilpah has 16 and Bilhah has 7, for a total of 23. Both of Jacob's wives, Leah and Rachel, have twice the number of children as their handmaids Zilpah and Bilhah.

Thus, the total number of Jacob's family who went to Egypt is 70, but even that number is somewhat off, for Israel has God to guide him and his family, so perhaps we should say there were 71.

Jacob and Joseph Finally Meet – 46:28–34

Judah was assigned to go ahead of the party traveling to Egypt to tell Joseph his family was arriving and to find where in Goshen they were to settle. It is most ironic that Judah, who occupied the fourth position in the family and who played the lead role in seeing that Joseph was separated from his father (37:26ff), is now given the lead role in acting as the mediator for reuniting his father with his long-missing son Joseph!

Jacob, in his earlier days, had known what it was like to send a party ahead to meet another family member; that is what happened when he prepared to meet his long-offended brother Esau (32:3). But this time the meeting would be one where he would be reunited with his son Joseph. In the separation between Jacob and Esau, the brothers were separated for some 20 years. This separation, between father and son, would last 22 years.

There is no record of the details of Jacob and Joseph's meeting. The text simply noted that Joseph harnessed his chariot—perhaps the chariot that had the license plate "*#2*"—and off he rode to meet his father after 22 years of separation. "When he saw him, he flung himself on his neck and wept on his neck steadily" (v. 29b). Israel did say this much to Joseph: "Now I can die, now that I have seen your face and know that you are alive" (v. 30).

Joseph took special care to instruct his family on matters of diplomatic procedures that needed to be observed. He would inform Pharaoh that his family had arrived in Goshen. Joseph would also tell Pharaoh that his family's vocation was of cattle- and sheep-tending. They were shepherds by trade; hence, the ideal territory for them to settle in would be Goshen, which allowed the family to provide for their cattle as well (vv. 31–32).

Thus, the family would do well to designate themselves to Pharaoh as his servants. Moreover, as shepherding was "an abomination" to the Egyptians, for some reason we have not been able to discover (unless it was that the expelled Hyksos invaders from Egypt who came from Asia in the 17th century were also called "shepherd kings"), the family had to make clear to Pharaoh that this was their honest vocation and had been for generations.

Nevertheless, this attitude among the Egyptians persisted, for later, when Moses requested of a later Pharaoh permission for the people to take a three-day journey into the desert to offer sacrifices, Moses stated his reason was because of the prevailing attitude of the Egyptians that offering sacrifices would be an "abomination" in the eyes of the Egyptians (Exodus 8:26). Both Gen. 46:34 and Exodus 8:26 use the Hebrew word *to`eba* for "abomination."

So, finally Joseph and Jacob met each other after a long separation!

Conclusions

1. The Lord identified himself to Jacob as "I am God" (46:3), the same name God used to identify himself to Moses (Exodus 3:6; 6:2, 6).

2. God promised his presence would go with Jacob as he went down to Egypt, so there would be no reason for being frightened.

3. The total number of descendants born to Jacob and his family at this point was 70.

4. God promised to bring the family of Jacob back to Canaan once again.

Lesson 10

Joseph Makes Pharaoh the Top Landowner in Egypt

Genesis 47:1–31

Sometime after Joseph had gotten his family settled in Goshen (47:11–12), he was able to turn his attention to the concerns of the nation of Egypt that he had begun to put his hand to some nine years ago after his appointment by Pharaoh as chief Czar of Distributions. Except that which Joseph had ordered set aside during the good years (see 41:35–37), and the food he had provided to his family, there was no food in Egypt or any of the surrounding countries (47:13). Joseph was the sole person in charge of the food distribution that was available anywhere.

After interpreting Pharaoh's dream, Joseph had advised hiring a wise man to oversee the administration of the food for the Egyptians (and for who knows for how many other countries where the famine was going on), but this was no small feat.

Joseph proposed that the farms in Egypt should grant to the government a fifth of all that the Egyptians raised during the seven good years. This collection amounted to a huge reservoir of grain, which no doubt was the wise and proper thing to do, for nothing else could have helped a starving generation except for the mountains of grain that had been stored up all over Egypt. His suggestion proved a lifesaver to thousands in Egypt and elsewhere. Joseph's plan seemed good to Pharaoh and his officials as Pharaoh added: "Can we find anyone like this man [Joseph], one in whom is the Spirit of God" (41:38). And this plan was good, wise and appropriate. Thus,

Pharaoh made Joseph the second-highest official in the land as he superintended the collection and then the distribution of this grain. Now Joseph was second only to Pharaoh himself (41:39–40).

Joseph threw himself wholeheartedly into his new appointment as commissioner and Grain Czar in Egypt. He traveled all over Egypt during those seven good years as he saw a fifth of the harvest piled up "like the sand of the sea" in amounts "beyond measure" near the farms that had produced this super-crop (41:49).

Curiously enough, the Bible is silent; it gives no judgment on who gave the authority Joseph used to charge the people money, then livestock, as payment for the grain. When both the people's silver and livestock had been exhausted, Joseph bought the farmers' land. But that too soon gave out, so last of all, when everything else was gone, he the people became Pharaoh's slaves. Joseph ended up instituting an oppressive set of controls over the distribution of grain for the remaining years of the famine. Egypt went from being a nation that enjoyed private ownership of wealth, possessions, and land to one of complete vassalage and bondage to the crown.

To review this serious matter, note that Joseph continued charging the Egyptians who came to him for the grain they received until all their money was gone. Then he accepted their cattle and livestock in exchange for grain until all those resources were also gone. When they had nothing else to trade with, Joseph accepted their lands and farms, and ultimately the Egyptians' own labor-power as payment. In the meantime, Pharaoh became fabulously rich while the nation of Egypt grew impoverished!

But nowhere in the biblical narrative is there a divine directive instructing Joseph how to distribute the grain, or the way he outlined it for Pharaoh. Where was God in Joseph's whole scheme of paying for the grain? It did not seem possible to assume the absence of divine authorization can be taken as tacit or an implied divine permission for Joseph to go ahead and do so. It is important to distinguish between what the Bible *records* as happening and what it *teaches*. As Terence Fretheim noted in his commentary of Genesis,

> As Joseph made "slaves" of the Egyptians (though not to himself), so the later Pharaohs—who do not have the wisdom and commitment of Joseph—will make "slaves" of [Joseph's] family. … While we cannot be certain, this reversal raises the question of whether the later Pharaohs extended Joseph's economic policy to include the Israelites.[1]

Joseph Introduces Five of His Brothers to Pharaoh – 47:1–6

After the family of Jacob was settled in Goshen, Joseph chose five of his eleven brothers to go meet Pharaoh. In his speech to Joseph (v. 5), he placed Joseph's father before his brothers, but neither party mentioned any daughters or grandkids as being part of the family! Why did he choose only five (v. 2)? We do not know who was chosen and why.

Joseph had rightly told his brothers that when they met Pharaoh, he would ask their occupation, and they should reply, "We are cattle-breeders," for shepherds were an abomination to the Egyptians (46:31–34). But the brothers did not heed Joseph's warning and said they were "shepherds." However, Pharaoh did not make any special point out of their reply, so all was safe for the moment. Three times they called themselves Pharaoh's "servants" (47:3–4). They requested that they be permitted to dwell in the land of Goshen. Pharaoh graciously said the land was open to them and they could dwell in the choice parts of the land (vv. 5–6).

---

1. Terence Fretheim, "The Book of Genesis: Introduction, and Reflections," in *The New Interpreter's Bible, Vol. 1* (Nashville: TN: Abingdon Press, 1994). 655.

Joseph Introduces His Father Jacob to Pharaoh – 47:7–12

When Joseph presented Jacob to Pharaoh (v. 7), Jacob immediately "blessed" this foreign monarch not once but twice (v. 10). Jacob, who may initially seem to be in a position much inferior to Pharaoh, nevertheless blessed the one who outwardly appeared to be superior! Perhaps that blessing was for Pharaoh to have a long life. If so, that would explain why Pharaoh asked in the next verse (v. 8), "How many years have you lived?"

Jacob answered that he had journeyed in life for 130 years, but his life had been few in comparison to those of his fathers, and they had been difficult years as well (v. 9). Jacob would live for yet another 17 years, for a total of 147 years (v. 28), compared to the 180 years of his father Isaac (35:28) and the 175 of his grandfather Abraham (25:7).

Jacob concluded by blessing Pharaoh once more, and then he left the palace (v. 10) to return to the place in Goshen where Joseph had settled his family. This site was in "the region of Ramesses," which is usually identified with Qantir or Tanis in the northeastern delta of the Nile (v. 11). Joseph provided even more for his brothers than their "sojourning" in Goshen; he gave them "property" (Hebrew *'ahuzzah*), which is unlike property transmitted by inheritance (*nahala*). But the property the brothers receive is what God had promised to Jacob, when he promised to make him a great nation (46:3); it is property given by a Sovereign! That is why the verb *natan*, "to give," is most often connected with this type of property.

Joseph's Agrarian Farm Program – 47:13–26

The famine was every bit as formidable as the Lord had indicated in Pharaoh's dream. No food was available anywhere in Egypt or Canaan (v. 13). In order to get food, Joseph took from the people their money (v. 14), later on he took their livestock (vv. 15–17), and in the end he took the land they had formerly used to grow super crop of grain (vv. 18–21). The famine was affecting Canaan just as badly as it was affecting Egypt.

Should Joseph then be seen as a callous, unethical taskmaster who was out to strip the people of Egypt of all they had possessed? It is true that after the famine had ended, Joseph gave them enough seed to sow their fields, thereby allowing the Egyptians to use the farms they had already given to Pharaoh in order to get grain, even though they had forfeited total ownership of that land. The new rule was that these farmers could keep 80% of their harvest and give just 20% to Pharaoh, which both parties agreed to.

The Egyptian people seemed grateful to Joseph for this ruling, for they told him, "You have rescued our lives" (47:25). It is hard to tell when in Egypt's history this land-reform system took place, but most Egyptologists think it was the period following the expulsion of the Hyksos and the beginning of the 18th Dynasty (ca. 1550 B.C.E.). As archeologist Roland de Vaux noted, the measures introduced into Egypt were the very ones the prophet Samuel condemned when the people wanted to have a king in Israel. He warned that if they persisted in wanting to have a king rule over them, then he would take over their farmlands, take a tithe from their crops, and make slaves of their sons and daughters (1 Samuel 8:13–16).[2] They did not care, so that is what happened.

Joseph Hears His Father's Final Request – 47:27–31

So, Israel settled down in Egypt with the promised blessing of God continuing to provide for them. Again, the text mentions that Jacob and his family were given property (11, 27) in the region of

---

2. Roland de Vaux, *The Early History of Israel* (London: Darton, Longman & Todd, 1978), 306–7.

Ramesses. Moreover, the family became "fruitful and [they] became very numerous" (v. 27). Nothing can stop the promises of God, neither new geography, the disaster of a famine, or the hateful actions of Joseph's own brothers.

We are not given any information on what happened during Jacob's final 17 years of life in Egypt. He lived to be 147 years old.

Israel had one more request to make of his son Joseph. Jacob wanted to be buried with his ancestors (v. 30). As he stated in Genesis 50:5, "bury me in the tomb I hewed out for myself." Jacob wanted to "be gathered to his kin" just as Abraham was (Gen. 25:8), Ishmael was (25:17), Isaac was (35:29), and now Jacob would be (49:29, 33). To guarantee Joseph would carry through on this, Jacob asked him to place his hand under Jacob's thigh. Jacob asked Joseph to swear to do this after he died, for Egypt was not the permanent place for the people of Israel. Anyway, the transport of his corpse back to his homeland was a sentimental request; moreover, Egypt was only a temporary shelter for the people of the promise (v. 31).

Conclusions

1. Jacob's arrival in Egypt brought to an end some 22 years of mourning for his son Joseph. He found him fully alive and graciously endowed by the God of all promises and plans for the future.

2. Joseph introduced his father Israel to Pharaoh, who outwardly was regarded as the leader of the mightiest empire even seen up to that day. But what Pharaoh did not realize was that Jacob had been given promises about his future and that of his family that easily outclassed anything he knew in his Egyptian empire.

3. Joseph set up an agrarian policy that took away from the Egyptians their freedoms and ownership of their wealth, lands and possessions.

4. Jacob blessed Pharaoh thrice, showing that any and all gifts come from the father of all mercies and lights in heaven above.

Joseph Visits His Ailing Father

Genesis 48:1–22

It seems the years of famine had passed by now. Jacob had long since arrived in Egypt, but he was feeling his infirmities and was bedridden (v. 1). However, when he was told that Joseph had come to see him, he "rallied his strength and sat up on the bed" (v. 2).

Joseph had also brought his two sons, Manasseh and Ephraim, along to see his father. We are not told what had caused his illness. It was not said to be terminal, but Jacob's condition was serious enough to merit notifying Joseph that his father was sick and summon him to Goshen. Evidently, from this note, Joseph did not reside with his family in Goshen; he no doubt stayed close to the palace where his brothers met him in his own house when they first came to Egypt.

When Joseph presented his sons to Jacob, he introduced them in birth order, Manasseh and Ephraim. Their birth had been described before the seven-year famine begun (41:50–52), but though Joseph had been reunited with Jacob sometime after the first two years of famine (46:29), the text gives no indication the boys' grandfather had ever met them. If so, why did Joseph take so long to show these two grandsons to him? Jacob did not recognize them: "Who are these?" (48:8). Was this because of his blindness, or because Joseph had never taken his sons to see their grandfather?

"Someone informed Jacob, 'Your son Joseph has come to you'" (v. 2). Was this a hired courtier, who made this announcement as

Joseph arrived in the village of Avaris? Again, there is no explanatory word. But we are told Jacob rallied his strength and sat up in his bed. This must have taken a good bit of effort, for it was noteworthy enough to be mentioned. This, then, will be the background against which this passage was written.

The Initial Presentation of Joseph's Two Sons – 48:1–7

Jacob and Joseph began their conversation with his father by taking a trip down memory lane of a key event from many years ago. The events of recent years had brought back to Jacob's mind the time long ago when God had appeared to him at Luz (later known as Bethel; Gen. 35:9–15). Jacob repeated the words God had given him on this occasion almost verbatim, with one variation. However, even in these small variations we the readers can often see Jacob's assessment of the divine promise.

In Genesis 35:11, the Lord had said: "Be fruitful and increase in number. A nation and a community of nations will come from your body." The difference is that when Jacob retold the story to Joseph, he changed the verbal imperatives in his statement to emphasize the part God will play in doing all he has promised:

> "I [the LORD] am going to make you fruitful and I will increase your number. I will make you a community of peoples, and I will give this land as an everlasting possession to your descendants after you." (48:5)

The difference that Jacob brings out in his retelling of this promise is that it is God himself who will bring to pass all he has promised. Indeed, all that has happened to the house of Jacob has all been a part of his plan and has been intended by the Lord "for good" (50:20).

Also note one other key difference between what God had said at that time in Luz and what Jacob now repeated: The Lord had promised "kings will come from your body" (35:11; see 17:6, 16) when Jacob was in Luz, but Jacob didn't mention that here. The reason for this may be because the stress on the future role of Judah in his kingship slot is now held in abeyance until that truth can be featured (in Gen. 49). It is interesting to see that Judah has risen in prominence over firstborn Reuben, presumably from the role he has assumed in leading his brothers back to Egypt for grain a second time.

Significantly, Jacob did not puff himself up by telling Joseph, "Son. Let me tell you what God did for *me* back there in Luz." Instead, he emphasized, "Son, let me tell you what our *God* promised in his great promises to our family and our families to come. The people of Israel did become "fruitful" and "numerous" in Egypt (47:27, 48:4). They have acquired land in Egypt, but this land was not like the land in Canaan promised at Luz, for this "inheritance" in Canaan would be an "everlasting inheritance."

After talking for a while on God's actions on their behalf in the past (48:3–4), Jacob turned to the future (vv. 5–6). Surprisingly, Jacob elevated Joseph's two sons from merely grandsons to two more of his own children. Jacob chose two of his oldest children, Reuben and Simeon, as comparisons for what he was about to do. Manasseh and Ephraim would now be called Jacob's "children," and Jacob would also be called "their father." Just as his other twelve sons called him "father," they would do likewise.

As an aside, what Jacob did has been compared to Law 170 in the Code of Hammurabi, that if the father during his lifetime ever said, 'My children!' to the children born to him by a slave, they were then counted as equal with children of his first wife. It's like saying Jacob had adopted Joseph's sons. Of course, they remained with their parents, but Jacob's declaration gave both Manasseh and Ephraim full legitimacy as part of the twelve tribes of Israel.

Jacob never paused to say why he did this, or even why he chose Joseph's sons over the 51 other grandsons he also had at that time. But also notice that in so doing, Jacob elevated Joseph an equal level with himself, for Joseph became one of the ancestral fathers of the tribes of Israel. Any additional children born to Joseph would be Joseph's children (v. 6). Any subsequent children of Joseph would come under the privileges and territory given to Ephraim and Manasseh.

In v. 7 Jacob again in his conversation with Joseph lapsed back into the past event of the death of his beloved Rachel as they journeyed from Paddan-Aram to Canaan (35:16–20). Why this came to Jacob's mind at this time is not clear. It may be that Rachel's prayer at the birth of Joseph ("May the LORD add to me another son," 30:24b) was answered not only by the birth of Benjamin but perhaps again by the birth of Manasseh and Ephraim.

Jacob Blesses Ephraim and Manasseh at Their Presentation – 48:8–16

Verse 10 informs us that Jacob's eyesight was failing him so badly that he was not able to see. We are told in Genesis 46:5 that Jacob knew Joseph had two sons who were born to him in Egypt and knew their names. It seems, however, that even though Jacob's eyesight was failing, he was not totally blind, for he could differentiate between the boys. Other interpreters have reminded us that the request for the names of boys is somewhat similar to the prelude and formula used at an infant baptism ("What name is given to this child?") or the question that is asked at a wedding ("Who giveth this woman to this man?").

Joseph responded, "My sons are these" (v. 9). With this, Joseph brought his sons right up to the arms of Jacob, and he kissed and embraced Joseph's two sons (v. 10). Then Jacob seemed to pause, for he then addressed Joseph and expressed his delight on "seeing" his son Joseph once again. Jacob also expressed his joy in being able to live so long so that he could see even Joseph's sons (v. 11). Jacob was the only patriarch who was able to meet and have any dealings with his grandchildren.

Some think Manasseh and Ephraim must have been relatively young in years, for Joseph removed his two boys from sitting on Jacob's knees and bowed before his father (v. 12). But they must not be regarded as being too small or young, for they had been born to Joseph before Jacob came to Egypt 17 years ago. So, they were at least teenagers at this point. Jacob never bowed before Joseph as in his dream long ago; but now his son, the second-most-powerful man in Egypt, amazingly bowed him (v. 12b).

For a second time, Joseph brought his two sons to the side of Jacob's bed (vv. 10, 13). He positioned his second-born son on Jacob's left hand and Manasseh, his firstborn, on Jacob's right hand, thinking Jacob's right hand of blessing would fall on his firstborn (v. 13). But Jacob surprised all present by crossing his hands and placing his right hand on the younger boy, Ephraim (v. 14). We do not know why, but this was not the first time a firstborn had been passed over in a paternal blessing. Consider these cases: Ishmael,

Esau, Reuben, Zerah. In some cases, the reason was because of the eldest son's behavior, such as in Reuben's case, but here we do not know the reason.

Jacob pronounced a blessing on the two grandsons, whom he had just named as his own sons (vv. 15–16). His blessing was exhibited in three parts: an invocation to God (v. 15), the actual prayer of blessing (v. 16b), and the results of the blessing and prayer (v. 16c–d). Jacob began by bearing witness to the way his father and grandfather had lived before God. Jacob shifted from using the past tense with his older relatives to participles ("God has been shepherding," "God has been delivering") when referring to his own life. So, from Rebekah's womb to Jacob's deathbed, God had been there for him all the way! After referring to "God" (v. 15b), Jacob moved easily to "the Angel" (v. 16a), who led him all his life. Jacob and his family had also encountered an angel several times. Twice an angel had attended to Hagar and her son (16:7–11; 21:17). An angel interrupted and impeded the use of Abraham's knife extended over Isaac's body (22:11–18) and helped guide Abraham's servant in his quest for a bride for Isaac in a foreign territory (24:7, 40). Jacob encountered an angel as he prepared to leave Laban (31:11), and he wrestled with an Angel (32:24–30) who left him impaired in his hip. Is it any wonder that Jacob said an angel delivered him "from every distress" (v. 16a)?

Jacob ended by asking God to not only bless the two boys, but to let his name live on in them, as it had in the names of his fathers, Abraham and Isaac. May the boys "multiply exceedingly in the land" (v. 16d).

Jacob Rejects Joseph's Correction at the Blessing – 48:17–22

Joseph assumed that because of his father's poor eyesight, Jacob had not noticed that he had presumably crossed his hands accidentally over the heads he was blessing; he thought Jacob was confused over which was the firstborn. His father's whole method seemed wrong. So, he moved his father's hands to bless his firstborn. But Jacob refused to be corrected: "I know, my son, I know." Manasseh would also become a great people nevertheless, for his younger brother would become greater than he and his descendants would become a company of peoples (vv. 17–19).

Now, a second time, Jacob blessed his grandsons (v. 20). Then Jacob announced it was time for him to die. He told to his family he believed God would bring them all back to the land of Canaan that God had long ago promised to give to their fathers (v. 21).

In conclusion, Jacob gave Joseph a piece of property above and beyond what Jacob gave his other children. Exactly where that land was located and when he had captured it from the Amorites, no one seems to know. The best sense we can make of v. 22 is that this land is connected with some conquest near Shechem, for later in history, Joshua led a covenant renewal at Shechem (Joshua 24), but there is no record that Joshua ever personally conquered it or led the troops of Israel. It seems, then, that once again Jacob gave an extra gift to Joseph—the first gift he gave him was a multicolored coat, and now this property in Shechem. So, there must have been a pre-Mosaic conquest of Shechem not recorded in Scripture except for this enigmatic note.

Conclusions

1. At the final visit of Joseph with his father Jacob in Goshen, he took his two sons, Manasseh and Ephraim, so that his father could bless his grandsons in his final minutes on earth.

2. Jacob recalled to Joseph the time when El-Shaddai, "God Almighty," met him at Luz. Jacob repeated God's blessing of his plan to make Jacob's seed prolific and numerous and give them the land of Canaan.

3. Jacob announced that Ephraim and Manasseh would be counted as his own children.

4. In his formal blessing of them, Jacob appealed to the God who had guided the footsteps of his grandfather Abraham and his father Isaac, and who in his lifetime had delivered him from every distress. He prayed that the Lord would live on in the lives of Joseph's two sons and that they would multiply exceedingly.

Lesson 12

Jacob Blesses His Twelve Sons

Genesis 49:1–33

Joseph was summoned for the last time to his father's side. Jacob intended to bless all of his children before he died (49:1). Jacob had already blessed Pharaoh (47:7–10), his son Joseph (48:15), and Joseph's two sons Ephraim and Manasseh (48:20). Now it remained for Jacob to give all his sons a blessing before he passed on to his eternal reward, so the sons of Jacob were all told to "gather" around him and "assemble" around him so they could "listen" and hear what he had to say (49:2).

The purpose of this gathering of his sons was, Jacob said, "so I can tell you what will happen to you in days to come/in the last days." (v. 1b). The expression "in the last days" appeared in an introduction to two other poems in the *Pentateuch* besides the blessing of Jacob (49:1–28): "The Burdens of Balaam" (Numbers 24:14–24) and "The Last Words of Moses" (Deuteronomy 31:29). In these three poems, the expression "in the last days" could refer to the future deliverance by the Messiah of Abraham's seed. At the center of all three poems where this expression occurs, is a word about a coming King (Gen. 49:10; Num. 24:7; Deut. 33:5), who is connected with the house of Judah and with the coming Messiah, i.e., Yeshua.

The author of this text clearly took pains to make sure we the readers understood that Jacob's words were about God's "blessing," which has been the overall theme and central concern for the book of Genesis ever since it opened its message in Genesis 1:28. To the twelve sons, "when he blessed them, giving each the blessing appropriate to him" (49:28).

The order of the blessing of the sons mostly follows their birth order. First, Jacob lists the sons of Leah in their order of birth: Reuben (vv. 3–4), Simeon and Levi are grouped together (vv. 5–7), Judah (vv. 8–12), Zebulun (v. 13), and Issachar (vv. 14–15). Then there follows the list of the sons of handmaidens: Bilhah gives birth to Dan (vv. 16–17), and Zilpah gives birth to Gad (vv. 18–19) and Asher (v. 20). Bilhah gives birth later on to a second son named Naphtali (v. 21). Then there follow the sons born to Jacob's favorite wife Rachel: Joseph (vv. 22–26) and Benjamin (v. 27). Let us examine this telling of what will take place.

Reuben – 49:3–4

There is quite of bit of wordplay in Jacob's words of blessing for most of his children, especially in the more cryptic and terse forms of blessing for some of the sons. Jacob began by acknowledging that Reuben was his firstborn and therefore the sign of Jacob's strength and his might. As such, Reuben excelled in power and honor for a time; however, Reuben would now no longer excel, for he [had gone] onto [Jacob's] couch and defiled it" by sleeping with his father's concubine Bilhah (35:22). Because of this blatant sin, Jacob stripped Reuben of his birthright as his firstborn. The writer of the book of Chronicles made this important comment:

> [Reuben] was the firstborn, but [when] he defiled his father's marriage bed, his rights as firstborn were given to the sons of Joseph son of Israel; so he could not be listed in the genealogical record in accordance with his birthright, and though Judah was the strongest of his brothers and a ruler came from him, the rights of the firstborn belonged to Joseph." (1 Chronicles 5:1–2)

Simeon and Levi – Cursed Be Their Anger – 49:5–7

These two brothers are grouped together because the two of them were the instigators of the slaughter of the citizens of the city of Shechem (34:25) for the pagan son of the leader of that city raped their sister Dinah. As a result of this outrage, these two brothers took it upon themselves to cause a genocide in that town. Therefore, Jacob would cede no territory to either of these sons, for they attacked a defenseless city and the Shechemites when they were still hurting from the circumcision they had agreed to. Instead of receiving a blessing, Simeon and Levi and their tribes would be scattered and dispersed throughout Israel (49:7).

Judah – A Scepter and Ruler's Staff – 49:8–12

After Jacob had dismissed the three older sons, he proceeded to predict a future for Judah that would give him preeminence over his brothers (v. 8). Judah's brothers would end up praising him, for he would have the dominant hand over all his enemies. In effect, it would have seemed Judah was given the right of the firstborn that had been stripped from Reuben and was passed over the heads of Levi and Simeon (1 Chronicles 5:1–2), but actually that right of the firstborn was given to Joseph (Gen. 48:5). However, even though Judah was not given that right of the firstborn, he was given a role of dominance over all the other eleven tribes. Judah was named the "strongest" over his brothers; thus, Judah became the heir to the throne. Is this not what Psalm 78:67–68 teaches:

"Then [the LORD] rejected the tents of Joseph, he did not choose the tribe of Ephraim; but he chose the tribe of Judah, Mount Zion, which he loved."

Jacob's words about Judah did not include the imagery found in many of the blessings of the other sons, for even though it was set in poetic images, Jacob's words were comparatively at times much more transparent than many of the images used with some of the other brothers. Moreover, what had happened to Joseph in his dreams (where his brothers bowed down to him) seemed to be now transferred to Judah's household in the future coming days until Messiah came.

Judah is pictured as a "young lion" (v. 9) sleeping in his den just after he had taken his prey. This picture is completed in v. 10, which describes the warrior as a king, i.e., the king who holds the scepter and ruler's staff. Jacob, therefore, is announcing that Judah will hold the royal status and dominion "until he to whom it belongs shall come" (v. 10b).

Some English versions leave untranslated the Hebrew word *Shiloh* in this verse, but the Hebrew expression may be a cipher that when translated means "the One to whom it belongs." When left untranslated, as in the KJV ("until Shiloh come"), it becomes an even stranger reading, for it combines the feminine subject "Shiloh" with a masculine verb "come." Elsewhere in the Bible, Shiloh is only a place name and does not represent an individual.

The Qumran community of the Dead Sea Scrolls had no doubt as to the meaning of Genesis 49:10, for in the 4Q Patriarchal Blessings manuscript, they interpreted Genesis 49:10 this way:

> "A ruler shall [not] depart from the tribe of Judah when Israel has dominion. [And] the one who sits on the throne of David [shall never] be cut off, because the 'ruler's staff' is the covenant of the kingdom, and the thousands of Israel [are] 'the feet,' until The

Righteous Messiah, the Branch of David has come. For to Him and to His seed the covenant of the kingdom of His people has been given for the eternal generations, because He has kept [...] the Law with the men of Yahad. For [...] the obedience of the people is the assembly of men of [...] he gave."[1]

Just as amazing is the fact about this one who is to come from the line of David that "the obedience of the nations [will] be his" (v. 10b). Note Jacob used the plural "nations," suggesting this kingship will reach far beyond Israel's borders. Indeed, it included in his promise-plan that his promise would make them into "a community of peoples" (Gen. 28:3, 48:4). This identical thought appeared in Psalm 2:8, where God "will make the nations [Israel's] inheritance. Even Daniel 7:13–14 made the same point, for to the Son of Man "was given authority, glory, sovereign power; all peoples, nations, and men of every language [would] worship him."

The images of prosperity and abundance continued in vv. 11–12. There the donkey would be tethered to the choicest of vines, and clothes would be washed in grape juice. In other words, the produce of the fields was so plentiful that beasts of burden could be hitched up to these vines, and wine would be so plentiful that it would be used in place of water to wash clothes.

Verse 12 picks up the picture of the king of Judah whose eyes are darker than wine and his teeth are whiter than milk. The picture is one of opulence and wealth. The future, in other words, would be most bright!

---

1. Michael Wise, Martin Abegg, Jr., and Edward Cook, *The Dead Sea Scrolls: A New Translation* (San Francisco: HarperSanFrancisco, 1996), 177.

Zebulun – A Haven for Ships – 49:13

For some reason, the order of birth is interrupted (as seen in Gen. 29–30), for the next son ought to have been either Dan, Bilhah's first son, or Issachar, Leah's fifth son. Instead, Jacob spoke of Zebulun, the tenth son overall and Leah's sixth and last son, thus jumping ahead of Issachar and transposing the position of the two brothers. Jacob, of course, must have had in mind to list first of all the six sons of Leah together, but he reversed the positions of Zebulun and Issachar, Leah's sixth and fifth sons, respectively. There is one other place in the Bible where this switch takes place—Deuteronomy 33:18 in "The Blessing of Moses," where Zebulun, the sixth son, once again is put in the fifth place as Issachar is moved from his birth-position as son number five. Some explain this repositioning as an attempt to get Zebulun (now made Leah's fifth son) parallel with Dan (who in Gen. 29–30 is listed as Jacob's fifth son), since both sons have a connection with the sea and the coastline!

Zebulun's territory did not actually touch the coast of the Mediterranean Sea (Joshua 19:10–16), but it would go almost as far as Sidon. In fact, Sidon may be taken as a collective term for all of Phoenicia, and if so, then its land extends into the Plain of Acco. Zebulun means a "lofty abode," which may point to the fact that this land will extend far beyond its borders one day!

Issachar – A Resting Place – 49:14–15

The name Issachar (Hebrew *yissakar*) is a play on the word for "wages" (*sakar*). He is pictured here as a strong donkey that sees a land where rest would be good, so he willingly shoulders the burden.

Dan – A Viper That Bites – 49:16–17

The son named Dan's name is a wordplay on the Hebrew *yadin*, meaning "he will judge." Thus, Dan will provide from this one tribe justice for all his people. Moreover, Dan is likened to a snake that attacks the heels of the horse that goes along the path. This word, however, ends positively: "I will look for your deliverance, O LORD." There are two Ugaritic texts referring to horses being bitten by snakes, hence the appeal to God to rescue them from this affliction!

Gad – Delivered from Attack – 49:18–19

Gad settled on the east side of the Jordan where they often had to fight off Ammonite and desert attackers (Judges 5:17, 11:1–12:7). In fact, Gad was rebuked for remaining on the east side of the Jordan River and not showing up to help the brothers in other battles.

Asher – Provisions for a King – 49:20

Asher, meaning "happy" or "blessed," is so designated because of the agricultural bounty he receives. Asher occupies a particularly fertile piece of property on the slopes of the Galilean highlands. Asher is praised for the richness of his food, for the tribe would be able to provide well for any royal taste. In fact, the tribe of Asher may have provided a select culinary assortment of food for Solomon (1 Kings 4:7).

Naphtali – Bears Beautiful Fawns – 49:21

In predicting the future for Naphtali, he is declared to be productive and one who produces beautiful progeny. But the prophecy for Naphtali is brief, like some of the other words given to the brothers, that it is difficult to say whether Jacob's word here is positive or negative. Nevertheless, Naphtali seems to have lived a rather peaceful nomadic lifestyle as they subsequently became more settled and built new villages.

Joseph – Blessings Will Rest on His Head – 49:22–26

One might have guessed that Jacob would have much more to say about his favorite son Joseph, especially since it again includes a blessing for his two sons Ephraim and Manasseh. Jacob began by depicting Joseph as a "fruitful vine near a spring, whose branches climb over a wall" (v. 22). But Joseph had to contend with enemies, possibly such as those from his hostile brothers who "tried to do him in" (Hebrew *satam*) by shooting at him with arrows (v. 23). But the attack was fruitless, for his bow was steady and his arms limber (v. 24). Joseph easily defended himself because the hand of the Mighty One of Jacob and the Shepherd, who is the Rock of Israel, intervened (v. 24). Jacob used six times the word "blessings," the very theme of the book of Genesis (vv. 25–26b). Jacob concluded by praying the blessings promised to the patriarchs would rest on Joseph's head.

Benjamin – A Ravenous Wolf – 49:27

Benjamin is pictured as a wolf who shares in his lair the prey he has seized the night before. The Benjamite judge Ehud delivered Israel from the Moabite king Eglon (Judges 3:15–30), and the Benjamites defended themselves against the other eleven tribes of Israel in the civil war (Judg. 20:14–21).

Summary – 49:28

This verse summarizes vv. 1–27 by mentioning the word "blessing" three times. Previously Jacob had blessed Pharaoh (Gen. 47), then he blessed Joseph's two sons (Gen. 48), but finally he blessed all twelve of his children.

Burial Instructions for Jacob's Body – 49:29–33

As a final act, Jacob gave instructions concerning his burial. He knew that in a short time he would be gathered to his people. This expression, "gathered to his people," occurs ten times in Scripture (Gen. 25:8, 17; 35:29; 49:29, 33; Numbers 20:24, 27:13, 31:2; Deuteronomy 32:50), but only 49:29 uses the singular form for "people/kin"; the plural form appears everywhere else. This looks forward to the prospect of a real reunion with all the believing ancestors who have gone on before Jacob, so the later teaching on the resurrection of the body was not unanticipated!

Jacob is very specific about where he wants to be buried: "in the cave in the field of Machpelah, east of Mamre, in the Land of Canaan" (30, 32). That was the field Abraham had bargained with the Hittites to buy for an agreed-upon price (Gen. 23). Moreover, he is clear why he wants to be buried there: That is where Abraham, his wife Sarah, his son Isaac, Isaac's wife Rebekah, and Jacob's wife Leah are buried (v. 31).

With those instructions completed, Jacob "pulled up his feet into his bed and breathed his last and was gathered to his people" (v. 33b).

Conclusions

1. There can be no doubt about the fact that "blessing" was the main theme of the book of Genesis.

2. Nor can there be any doubt that God had for his own reasons chosen to bless the patriarchs and their descendants, the Israelites, as the channels through which the divine blessing would flow to all the world.

3. Nor can there be any doubt that it was the tribe of Judah who would receive the scepter of governing and ruling on the throne of Israel "until the One to whom it belonged came," i.e., the Messiah.

4. All the blessings of heaven above and the blessings of the depths below along with the blessings of the breast and womb would be available to Israel for their great prosperity and abundance.

Lesson 13

The Deaths of Jacob and Joseph, and Joseph's Forgiveness

Genesis 50:1–26

Rather remarkably, Joseph is the only son who is mentioned as mourning his father's death. Jacob had announced on an earlier occasion that Joseph would be the one who would close his father's eyes when he died (46:4), an honor typically reserved for the one who was closest to that person. But Joseph was truly heartbroken over his father's departure, for he "threw himself on his father and wept over him and kissed him (v. 1).

Then Joseph ordered his father's body embalmed, no doubt in the manner Egyptians cared for their own deceased persons. So significant is the death of Jacob that more than half of this final chapter is dedicated to describing all that went into the mourning for and burial of Jacob. The embalming process took "forty days" (v. 3), followed by an additional thirty days of mourning. The total number of days came to seventy days. Whether Pharaoh had the whole nation of Egypt enter into two-and-a-half months of mourning for the father of this foreigner who had risen to second-in-command is unknown, but certainly Pharaoh thought very highly of Joseph for what he had done for him and preserving Egypt during seven years of calamity. Who knows what might have happened without Joseph!

Acts of Sorrow and Laments for Jacob at His Death – 50:1–14

Just before Jacob died, he had given careful instructions that his body was to be taken back to Canaan so he could be buried there, the same place where his grandfather, Abraham, and his father, Isaac, were buried (49:29–32; 50:5). When Pharaoh heard Joseph's request on behalf of his father, Pharaoh allowed Joseph to honor his father's final request (50:4). In fact, Pharaoh arranged things for Jacob's funeral so that he was treated much like an Egyptian dignitary. Pharaoh ordered his officials— "the dignitaries of his court and all the dignitaries of Egypt"—to accompany Joseph and family to Canaan (v. 7). Moreover, Pharaoh equipped Joseph and his company with "chariots and horsemen," so the whole funeral cortege ended up being "a very large [and impressive] company" (v. 9). All this attracted the attention of the local Canaanites. This assemblage of so many persons of prestige and power must have been an awesome sight!

Joseph repeated to Pharaoh's representatives the oath Jacob had made him swear, but naturally and wisely, he left out at least two items in the original event. He said nothing about Jacob having him place his hand on his thigh (a custom that would have been totally unintelligible to Pharaoh). Also, he did not repeat Jacob's words about "Do not bury me in Egypt … [but] carry me out of Egypt." Jacob did not want to seem ungrateful to his host; it was just that God had previously given Abraham, Isaac, and Jacob the land of Canaan to inhabit and to be interred there. Pharaoh graciously granted Jacob and Joseph's request; anyway, Joseph had already promised to return to Egypt after his father's funeral (50:5c).

Actually, three different groups participated in Jacob's funeral procession: those who were high-ranking in Pharaoh's administration (v. 7), all the males in Jacob's family who were still alive (v. 8), and a military escort who rode along in their chariots and horsemen (v. 9). Later Israel would be pursued by an Egyptian retinue of chariots and horsemen, but for now this retinue would accompany Jacob's party.

This funeral march halted at Goren ha-Atad ("the threshing floor of Atad"), where they paused for seven days for an additional time of lament as Joseph mourned for his father and where, together, they raised "a loud and solemn lament" (v. 10). The location of this site has not been identified, but it is said to be "in the region of the Jordan," or "beyond the Jordan," i.e., in Transjordan, or East Jordan. But if this is the correct reading, it means this funeral procession did not take the ordinary route from Egypt into Canaan but for some reason took a route around the south end of the Dead Sea and ended up in Jordan—exactly the real estate Moses would end up leading the Israelites to cover before going forward to conquer Canaan. After the seven days of mourning, the whole retinue crossed the Jordan, or backtracked around the south end of the Dead Sea, to go to Hebron.

The inhabitants of the land of Canaan watched these proceedings for afar and remarked: "How grievously the Egyptians are mourning" (v. 11). Thus, the locals named that spot "Abel-Mizraim," meaning "mourning of the Egyptians." In doing all of this, Jacob's sons "expedited all [Jacob's] wishes" (v. 12). After the seven days of mourning, they carried Jacob to the cave of Machpelah, the plot of land Abraham had purchased long ago from Ephron the Hittite (v. 13; see Gen. 23). After burying his father, Joseph, and his brothers and all who had accompanied him, returned to Egypt (v. 14).

Acts of Forgiveness by Joseph to His Brothers at His Father's Death – 50:15–21

With the full realization that now that their father Jacob was dead and interred in Canaan, the issue was raised in their minds again: What if Joseph might hold it against them for hating him so violently (Gen. 37:4, 5, 8)? They felt they had to make amends somehow. But Joseph had not given the brothers any cause to Joseph to think they were in trouble with him. In fact, Joseph reassured them, "You intended to harm me, but God intended it for good to accomplish … the saving of many lives" (50:20; see 45:5). Here then was the central theme of the Joseph narrative: Behind all the events and human plans laid God's unchanging plan, stretching from the beginning of Genesis to this ending. God looked at what he had created, and it was very good (Gen. 1:4–31). Then through God's dealings with the Patriarchs and Joseph, our Lord continued to bring about his good plan as he remained faithful to his promises, for the God of gods and Lord of lords was by himself working all things for the good of those who love him and have been called according to his purpose (Romans 8:28).

When Joseph heard his brothers' plea for forgiveness and reconciliation, he wept (50:17c). Why Joseph reacted this way we do not know, but it may have been the natural outpouring of a ton of pent-up feelings that were all mixed up, suddenly let loose like a dam bursting. Instead of taking an adversarial stance, he "consoled them by speaking [to them] affectionately" (v. 21b). It is not certain why it took so long for the brothers to ask forgiveness, but their father's dying exhortation moved them to repent.

Joseph asked his brothers rhetorically, "Am I in the place of God?" (50:19). Once before, as noted, Joseph testified to the fact that his brothers were not the ones who sent him to Egypt, but it had been God who did so all along (45:7–8). Thus, the brothers' evil machinations actually turned out to be something beneficial God had done for Joseph. So, the point is this: His brothers really did commit an evil act against Joseph, but God used it for good! And the good that came out of it was "the survival of many people." Such a theme as the beneficent divine plan working through calamity and evil for good is by no means only found here in Joseph's story; consider other narratives that illustrate that same triumph of good over evil in the lives of Ruth, Daniel, Esther, even Judas Iscariot! In fact, one could say this is the message of the whole of Scripture—God's redemptive plan.

By this time, the seven-year famine was long past history, but Joseph continued to help his family while he lived with them in Egypt (v. 21).

Acts of Love as a Concluding Summary of Joseph's Life and Death – 50:22–26

Joseph lived a total of 110 years, 17 of which he had enjoyed as a growing boy in Canaan and 93 as an adult in Egypt. We are not given the dates of his brothers' deaths, so we don't know whether they outlived him or died before he did. But it is traditional to comment of Joseph's 110 years as being the ideal lifespan for an Egyptian—a life-span Joseph also shares with Joshua (Josh. 24:29). Joseph lived long enough to see his great-grandchildren through Ephraim and some great-grandsons through Manasseh—that is, the sons of Machir—begin to grow up (v. 23).

God had frequently made an oath to the Patriarchs to keep his promises to them. But now Joseph, seeing he was about to die, placed his brothers and all the men of Israel under oath to carry him back to the land of Canaan, just as they had carried their father Jacob (v. 24). Joseph saw a future day when God would come to the assistance of the sons of Israel (v. 25), just as they would also promise to carry Joseph's bones back to Canaan. Joseph repeated to the Israelites, "God will surely come to your aid, and then you must carry my bones up from this place [Egypt]" to Canaan (v. 25; see 41:32).

Conclusions

1. The promise-plan of God is the dominant theme of Genesis and the Bible. God will conclude in perfect form his promises to the three Patriarchs, Abraham, Isaac, and Jacob, who represent the Jewish line though which God's blessings will be shared with the whole world.

2. Joseph and the family carried Jacob's bones back to Canaan as they had sworn an oath to do, for they fully expected God to be faithful to this gift of the land of Canaan.

3. Joseph again graciously forgave his brothers for what they had done.

4. The brothers had meant their selling of their brother to be a riddance of one they hated, but God meant it for the saving of many peoples in a time of deep tragedy.

Printed in the United States
by Baker & Taylor Publisher Services